Grand Canyon Tips

The Local's Guide to Avoiding the
Crowds and Getting the Most Out of
Your Visit

Bruce Grubbs

Bright Angel Press

Flagstaff, Arizona

Grand Canyon Tips

The Local's Guide to Avoiding the Crowds and Getting the Most Out of Your Visit

Revised February 2018

Photographs, images, and illustrations by Bruce Grubbs unless otherwise credited

Bright Angel Press

Flagstaff, Arizona

www.BrightAngelPress.com

ISBN-13: 978-0-9899298-5-1

While every effort has been made to assure the accuracy of the information in this book, by using this book you take full responsibility for your own safety and recognize that outdoor activities may be hazardous.

Acknowledgments

Thanks to everyone who made this possible, not least to my Grand Canyon hiking and exploring partners over the years, for putting up with my incessant photography. And thanks to Peter Levine for his usual excellent job of copyediting. And finally, warmest thanks to Duart Martin for her unwavering support and encouragement.

Contents

Introduction

The purpose of this book is to share with you some tips on how to enjoy the Grand Canyon and avoid the crowds, based on my several decades of experience exploring the Canyon.

The Grand Canyon is one of the most popular tourist destinations on the planet, and it hosts more than five million visitors every year. At peak times, it can take several hours just to get through the lines at the entrance station, and then, be almost impossible to find a parking space. Popular viewpoints can be so crowded that it's even difficult to get to the rim for a good look.

Yet, at the same time the crowds are jostling for a view, with a little bit of effort you can find your own private spot along the rim to enjoy the ever-changing scene painted by light and shadow, and the stunning natural quiet of this immense chasm.

Using This Book

To get the most use out of this book, you should have it with you. I've deliberately kept the paperback book as small as possible by eliminating photos and keeping maps and graphics to a minimum, so you can just stuff it in your pocket or purse.

Even better, get the Kindle ebook edition and keep it on your phone or tablet. The Kindle edition was designed for both the gray-scale E Ink Kindle book readers as well as the color Fire tablets. And free Kindle Reading Apps are available for everything else, including iPhone, Android, Blackberry, Windows Phone, PC, and Mac. So you can have this little book handy on your phone or tablet and refer to it instantly when you're trying to find a place to eat, or the best viewpoint for sunrise.

If your curiosity is piqued and you want to learn more about the Grand Canyon's formation, geology, plants and animals, and human history, refer to my other book, *Grand Canyon Guide*, as well as my website, *ExploringGrandCanyon.info*.

Map of Grand Canyon Region

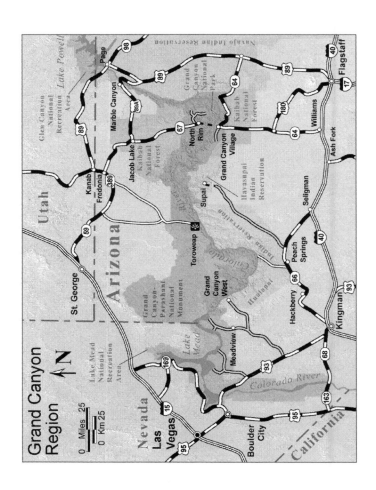

Stay Safe

Every year, a few people fall off the rim and die. Many more fall victim to dehydration and heat-related problems. Occasional visitors are bitten by wild animals, usually because they got too close when attempting to (illegally) feed them, or when taking a photo.

> **Tip**
>
> Don't have your vacation ruined by tragedy- use common sense and understand that the Grand Canyon is mostly a wilderness where the laws of nature rule.

Use Care Near the Rim

Only a tiny fraction of the Grand Canyon's more than 1,000 miles of rim are equipped with guard rails or walls. Yet, these improved viewpoints are where most people manage to fall off the rim, usually when showing off or from not paying attention while taking a photo. Respect the barriers if they are there, and don't climb on them or clown around.

All you have to do is take a short walk away from the major viewpoints to experience the wild rim of the Canyon. Use caution near the edge- what looks like a solid outcrop may actually be an overhanging ledge ready to break off. Sloping dirt terraces are especially treacherous. There is often only a thin layer of dirt or pebbles over a layer of rock, and the loose material can act as ball bearings and send you flying off the cliff below.

In the winter, snow and ice are often present along and just below the rim, on the steep north-facing slopes. Stay off these extremely slippery slopes!

Never throw anything off the rim or over a cliff, no matter where you are. There are hiking trails that pass below some of the viewpoints and nearby areas on the rim. There are also cross-country hiking routes throughout the canyon, so you can never tell when there may be people below, not to mention wildlife.

Avoid Heat Injury

Because of the high altitude and dry air, it is easy to become dehydrated, even during the winter. In the summer, when South Rim temperatures can reach 95°F (35°C) and humidity drops to less than 10%, your body loses moisture rapidly, often without noticeable sweating. Below the rim, the Canyon is much hotter- the temperature rises approximately five degrees for every thousand feet you descend, so the temperature at the Colorado River often reaches 120F during summer. In those conditions, you need about a gallon of water per day just to stay alive, and much more if you're doing strenuous exercise.

Dehydration can quickly lead to serious illness, in the form of heat exhaustion, which is debilitating, and sun stroke, which is a life-threatening medical emergency.

Because of the thin air at these altitudes (7,000 feet at the South Rim, and nearly 9,000 feet on the North Rim), ultraviolet radiation is intense from March through September and you can quickly receive a bad sunburn. Wear a sun hat and sun screen.

Tip

Never leave a pet in an unattended vehicle. The heat is lethal.

Wild Animals

It is extremely rare for wild animals to attack humans- driving to the park is far riskier than any threat from wild animals. But, always remember that wild animals are just that- wild. The Grand Canyon is a nature preserve, not a theme park. Never approach or feed any wild animal, no matter how cute or tame it may appear. Even rabbits will attack if they feel their young are threatened.

The Grand Canyon is home for a wide diversity of plants and animals- and that's the key word. This is their home and you are a temporary visitor. Treat their home with the same respect you would treat a friend's home. Don't litter or disturb vegetation, rocks, or artifacts of any kind. Leave everything as you found it and take only pictures.

Tip

Never, ever feed wild animals. You may think you're doing them a favor, but you're not. You're killing them. Human food is not good for wild animals, and they rapidly become dependent on handouts and lose the ability to fend for themselves. When winter and the off season arrives, they starve to death. For those reasons, it is illegal to feed wildlife.

In addition, rodents such as squirrels and mice often have fleas, which can carry plague. Although treatable with modern medicine, plague is still a nasty disease and getting a case will probably mess up your vacation.

Roosevelt elk and mule deer are common on both rims, and since hunting is not allowed in the park, these large and interesting animals are used to humans and don't regard us as a threat. They'll walk right through the campgrounds, saunter along the rim trails, and hang out on the edge of the park roads, creating huge traffic jams. Don't ever stop on the road to view wildlife or the Canyon, or for any reason short of an emergency. Doing so is very dangerous to other drivers. Always find a safe pullout and park so that your vehicle is completely clear of the roadway.

Tip

Never collect anything in the park- rocks, artifacts, firewood, or plants. Grand Canyon National Park is a nature preserve- help keep it unchanged for future generations and leave everything as you found it.

Wild Humans

During high season, Grand Canyon Village is a crowded little city, with all of the usual urban problems, including theft. Even the viewpoints and North Rim Village can be crowded, and all it takes is a careless moment to lose your valuables. Try to avoid leaving valuables of any kind in your vehicle, but if you must, make sure they are in the trunk or otherwise hidden. Lock your vehicle every time you leave it, even for a moment.

When and Where to Visit

Some visitors are surprised to find long lines and crowds at the Grand Canyon. Grand Canyon, as one of the Seven Natural Wonders of the World, is the second-most visited National Park in the United States. It is extremely popular not only with Americans, but also with tourists frrom all over the world, and is especially popular with Europeans and Asians.

Although the Grand Canyon is 277 river miles long and 10 to 20 miles wide and encompasses several thousand square miles (around 10,000 square kilometers), nearly all the visitors concentrate at Grand Canyon Village on the eastern end of the South Rim and Grand Canyon West at the far western end of the South Rim. Most of the Grand Canyon is remote wilderness and sees very few visitors- which is hard to believe when you're stuck in the South Rim entrance line for several hours.

Tip

The trick to having an enjoyable experience at the Grand Canyon is to avoid the times and places where the crowds congregate. To avoid the crowds at Grand Canyon Village, go in the winter. During high season, which is spring, summer, and fall, arrive at the park entrance by 9:00 AM. If you're staying in the park or nearby Tusayan, go to the popular viewpoints at sunrise instead of sunset. If you're willing to walk just a short distance, you can leave 90% of visitors behind even during peak times.

Visiting the Park

The best way to avoid crowds is to go during off season, which for the South Rim and Grand Canyon Village is winter, December through February. Although there is often snow on the rim, and nighttime temperatures dip into the teens Fahrenheit, days usually warm up into the 50's F and the southern sun is warm. Most days are clear, even during mid-winter. Snow storms usually last only a day or two, followed by a week or more of clear skies and sunny weather. As a bonus, the soft, low-angle winter light coupled with snow on the higher terraces really brings out the colors of the canyon rock formations.

Tip

There is one winter week that is NOT off season- Christmas to New Years Day. Avoid visiting during this time- entrance lines can be longer than during the summer.

Since North Rim Village is closed all winter, off season is shorter. A good time to visit is from May 15, when the road opens for the season, through early June. The crowds also thin out after the Labor Day holiday at the beginning of September. Although the park facilities, including Grand Canyon Lodge and North Rim Campground, close October 15, the North Rim actually stays open until November 15 or the first heavy snow, whichever comes first. So you can stay outside the park at Jacob Lake, Fredonia, Kanab, Marble Canyon, or Page, and do a day trip to the viewpoints at the North Rim.

Weekdays vs Weekends and Holidays

Because it is an international destination, the day of the week makes no difference to the numbers of people visiting Grand Canyon National Park. The three American summer holidays, Memorial Day, Fourth of July, and Labor Day do see an increase in visitation, so this is a good time to go somewhere else.

Supai

Since the only way to reach Supai Village is via horse or foot on the eight-mile long Hualapai Hilltop Trail, the Havasupai Reservation sees a tiny number of visitors compared to the other developed areas of the Grand Canyon. Still, Supai Village and the adjoining campgrounds occupy a small area at the bottom of a deep canyon, and the area is crowded during popular times such as Easter weekend. During Easter and to a lesser degree during the summer holidays, the campgrounds just downstream of Supai Village can be full to overflowing. Early spring and late fall are the best times to visit to avoid crowds, although the creek may be too cold to swim in.

Tip

If you want to stay in the small lodge in the village itself, make reservations as far in advance as you can, at http://www.havasupai-nsn.gov/tourism.html.

Grand Canyon West

Most visitors to this development on the far western end of the South Rim arrive as part of organized tour groups by bus or airplane from Las Vegas, Nevada. Since tour companies tend to book Las Vegas hotel rooms during the week when rates are deeply discounted, the peak days for Grand Canyon West are Monday-Thursday. If you're driving out to Grand Canyon West or booking a tour, try to visit on Friday, Saturday, or Sunday. Grand Canyon West is open all year and it is so popular with large tours from Las Vegas that there is no off season.

Tip

If you're driving to Grand Canyon West, arrive as early as you can. Grand Canyon West is open sunrise to sunset, and the helicopter tour companies generally start flying tours at 8:00 AM. I strongly recommend making advance reservations for helicopter flights, as large tour groups book these flights and it may be impossible to get on a flight without a reservation. See "Fly the Canyon" for contact information. The helicopter companies listed under "Las Vegas" all offer flights from Grand Canyon West, as well as Las Vegas.

Other Grand Canyon Destinations

The vast majority of visitors go to Grand Canyon Village on the South Rim in Grand Canyon National Park. The next most popular place is Grand Canyon West, on the Hualapai Indian Reservation at the far western end of the South Rim. North Rim Village, directly across the Canyon from Grand Canyon Village, hosts far fewer visitors, as does Supai Village in Havasu Canyon in the central portion of the South Rim. And both Grand Canyon-Parashant National Monument and Toroweap, reachable only via unpaved back roads, have very low visitation because relatively few visitors are willing to venture onto dirt roads and four-wheel-drive tracks. Even fewer people venture below the rim into the depths of the Grand Canyon, a vast wilderness which is accessible only by hiking or by running the Colorado River.

To put some numbers on it- each year, over 5,000,000 people visit Grand Canyon Village on the south Rim, about 1,000,000 visitors go to Grand Canyon West, and approximately 100,000 visit North Rim Village. These developed areas actually occupy a tiny fraction of the Grand Canyon country, so if you are able and willing to get off the beaten track (which means driving on remote dirt roads), you can easily spend days or weeks without seeing another visitor. These areas include the Kaibab National Forest adjacent to the national park on the South and North rims, Grand Canyon-Parashant National Monument, and several Wilderness Areas administered by the US Forest Service and the Bureau of Land Management.

12

Getting There

You'll need a car to get to the Grand Canyon, unless you arrive on an airplane or a bus as part of an organized tour group. There are no rental cars at the Grand Canyon- the nearest rental car agencies are located in Williams, Flagstaff, Kingman, and Phoenix.

> **Tip**
>
> **There is no scheduled airline service to the Grand Canyon.** The nearest cities with airline service are Page, Flagstaff, and Kingman, Arizona, and Las Vegas, Nevada. Grand Canyon West and Grand Canyon National Park airports are served only by tour and charter flights. Some airline tickets list your destination as Flagstaff-Grand Canyon, or Las Vegas-Grand Canyon, **but you will not land at Grand Canyon.**

The Grand Canyon runs generally east to west, which means the Canyon has two rims- the North Rim and the South Rim which both run the entire length of the canyon. But "North Rim" and "South Rim" are most commonly used to refer to the developed Grand Canyon Village area on the South Rim, and the developed North Rim Village area. Have a look at the Overview Map to see where these places are.

Be Prepared

The Grand Canyon is located in one of the most remote and least-populated portions of the 48 states. Services are very limited in Grand Canyon Village, even more so at North Rim Village, and non-existent elsewhere. Make sure your vehicle is in good condition by having a tune-up done before you head to the Canyon, especially if you're going to spend any time at the North Rim or exploring back roads. There is a service station in Grand Canyon Village, but it can only do minor repairs. Any major breakdown of your vehicle anywhere in the Grand Canyon region will mean a long and expensive tow to Flagstaff, Williams, Page, Arizona, or Kanab, Utah, for repairs.

Bring a spare set of car keys and give them to another member of your party. If you lock yourself out, it will take hours to get a locksmith.

> **Tip**
>
> Be cautious when using a GPS receiver to navigate in the Grand Canyon area. All of the roads on the plateaus surrounding the Grand Canyon are unpaved and mostly unmaintained, except for the Diamond Bar Road to Grand Canyon West, Supai Highway to Hualapai Trailhead, AZ 64 to Grand Canyon Village, and AZ 67 to North Rim Village. Many GPS receivers do not clearly indicate whether roads are paved, maintained gravel, or unmaintained two-track roads. Do not blindly follow your GPS receiver onto a dirt road unless you are intending to drive back roads and are prepared and equipped for that kind of driving.

Top off your gas tank when it reaches half full. Towns and gas stations can be 50 miles apart in Arizona. They may look close together on the highway map or your map app, but Arizona is a very large state and the maps are rendered at a much smaller scale than maps of the east coast states or Europe.

Winter often brings snowstorms at the high elevations of the Canyon rims. In fact, the North Rim is closed during the winter due to deep snow. Although the South Rim remains open all year, storms can temporarily close park roads. Be prepared for winter weather and road conditions by stoking your car with water, food, warm clothing, blankets, and tire chains (if appropriate for your vehicle.)

> **Tip**
>
> During the summer, carry several gallons of water in your car. In the case of a breakdown in a remote area, the summer heat will quickly kill you if you run out of water.

Check road conditions with the park at (928) 623-7594, or the Arizona road condition number, 511, or website, AZ511.com.

Drive Safely

Watch for elk when driving to the Grand Canyon, especially between sunset and sunrise. These very large deer are common in the forests surrounding the canyon, and if you hit one on the highway, the result is often fatal for the occupants of the vehicle.

Tip

Never stop on the road, outside or inside the national park, to view elk or any other animals. Doing so blocks the highway and creates an extreme hazard to other vehicles. Always find a pullout or wide shoulder and park completely off the road.

Driving to the South Rim

From Williams

Drive 63 miles north on AZ 64 and US 180 to the South Entrance Station just north of the gateway town of Tusayan.

Tip

You can do a loop drive from Williams, by driving north on AZ 64 east on Desert View Drive and AZ 64, south on US 89 (past the Wupataki and Sunset Crater national momuments turnoffs), and then west on I-40.

From Flagstaff

Drive 81 miles north on US 180 to the South Entrance Station just north of the gateway town of Tusayan.

From Cameron

Drive 55 miles west on AZ 64 to Grand Canyon Village. You'll pass through the East Entrance Station and enter the park just before Desert View. Continue 25 miles west on Desert View Drive to reach Grand Canyon Village.

Tip

You can do a loop drive from Flagstaff to the Grand Canyon and back via US 180, AZ 64, Desert View Drive, and US 89. US 89 passes the turnoffs to Wupatki and Sunset Crater national monuments, so it is easy to add them to your drive.

Other Ways to Reach Grand Canyon Village

Grand Canyon Railway offers service between Williams and Grand Canyon Village. www.thetrain.com, 800-THE-TRAIN

Arizona Shuttle offers ground shuttle service from Phoenix Sky Harbor Airport to Sedona, Flagstaff, and Tusayan near the South Rim. www.arizonashuttle.com, 800-888-2749

Because there are no rental cars at Grand Canyon Village, if you come by train or shuttle, you'll have to get around on the free park shuttles and by foot or bicycle (you can rent bicycles at Grand Canyon Visitor Center.) The Grand Canyon Railway terminal at Grand Canyon Village is just across the road from a stop on the Village Shuttle route. Arizona Shuttle drops you in Tusayan, just south of the South Entrance to the park. The free Tusayan Shuttle operates during the summer months, and connects with the rest of the shuttle system at Grand Canyon Visitor Center inside the park.

Xanterra, the operator of the lodges at Grand Canyon Village, offers taxi service between Grand Canyon National Park airport, and points in Tusayan and Grand Canyon Village. Call (928) 638-2822.

Getting Around Grand Canyon Village

When you enter the park, you'll be given a park guide with a map of Grand Canyon Village. The map shows the locations of the amenities and services in the village, including lodges, restaurants, stores and gift shops, and the main visitor center. The map also shows the free park shuttle routes and schedules, as well as the main parking lots.

Tip

Get a copy of the park guide online in advance of your visit to help you plan: http://www.nps.gov/grca/learn/news/upload/sr-pocket-map.pdf

Free Shuttle System

You can transfer between all the free park shuttles except Hermit Shuttle at Grand Canyon Visitor Center which is just inside the park after you pass through the South Entrance Station. The Hermit Shuttle transfer point is at Bright Angel Trailhead at the west end of the Village Shuttle loop.

Tip

Once you arrive at Grand Canyon Village, park your car and use the free shuttle bus to get around the South Rim. There is a shuttle route around Grand Canyon Village and a shuttle to the Kaibab Trailhead and Yaki Point. Except during the winter, the Hermit Shuttle runs from the transfer point at Bright Angel Traihead to Hermits Rest and the Hermit Road. During the summer, the Tusayan Shuttle connects Tusayan with the Grand Canyon Visitor Center inside the park. During the summer, the shuttles can be standing room only but riding the shuttles still beats hunting endlessly for a parking spot.

Bicycles

Bicycles are welcome on the free shuttle buses, and you can bring your own or rent one at Grand Canyon Visitor Center. Bicycles are welcome on all park roads and on the Greenway Trail through the Village, and on the east end of the Rim Trail from near Pipe Creek Vista to South Kaibab Trailhead. Bikes are not allowed on any other trails within the park, but there is virtually unlimited riding on two-track and maintained dirt roads in the Kaibab National Forest, which adjoins the national park on both the South and North rims.

If you're a mountain biker, the Arizona Trail, in the Kaibab National Forest on both rims, offers some scenic singletrack.

Biking is a great way to get around Grand Canyon Village, especially combined with the free shuttles. An enjoyable road ride is Hermit Road from Grand Canyon Village to Hermits Rest, which is closed to private vehicles March through November.

Parking

Many of the parking lots in Grand Canyon Village fill early in the day during peak season- even the large ones at Grand Canyon Visitor Center. If you can't find a spot there, drive through the village to Maswik Lodge. You can almost always find a spot in this large, out-of-the way parking lot. Then use the Village Shuttle to get around.

Tip

If you're driving a motorhome or pulling a trailer, head straight for the large parking lot at Maswick Lodge, which has RV spaces.

Driving to the North Rim

The North Rim is closed from October 15 to May 15 each year, but the road to North Rim Village stays open until November 15 or the first heavy snow. The Cape Royal Road closes sometime after October 15, depending on traffic and snowfall, but always by November 15.

Because all North Rim facilities and the campground close October 15, any visits after that have to be day trips, but this is a very quiet time to visit the North Rim. Go the third week of October to catch the last of the fall color in the quaking aspen groves.

Tip

Top off your fuel tank at Jacob Lake- it's nearly a 90-mile round trip to the North Rim and back, not counting any side trips you take. Also, walk over to the Forest Service Visitor Center for an overview of the North Rim and the Kaibab Plateau. You can also pick up maps and books.

From Flagstaff

Drive 109 miles north on US 89. Turn left on US 89A, and drive 55 miles north to Jacob Lake. Turn left on AZ 67, and drive 43 miles, passing the North Entrance Station, to North Rim Village.

From Kanab Utah

Drive 37 miles south on US 89A to Jacob Lake. (There is a Forest Service Visitor Center at Jacob Lake.) Turn right on AZ 67, and drive 43 miles, passing the North Entrance Station, to North Rim Village.

From Grand Canyon Village

From Grand Canyon Visitor Center drive about a mile, then turn left (east) on Desert View Drive. Continue 55 miles to Cameron, then turn left (north) on US 89. Drive 58 miles, then turn left on AZ 89A. Drive 53 miles to Jacob Lake, then turn left on AZ 67 and drive 43 miles, past the North Rim Entrance Station, to North Rim Village.

Other Ways to Reach North Rim Village

Trans Canyon Shuttle offers ground shuttle service between Grand Canyon Village, Marble Canyon, and North Rim Village. www.trans-canyonshuttle.com, 877-638-2820

Once at North Rim Village, you'll be on foot, since there is no public transportation. This limits you to the village area, and you'll have no way to reach Point Imperial or Cape Royal.

Supai

From Flagstaff

Drive 70 miles west on I-40, then exit onto historic AZ 66 at Seligman. Drive 30 miles west, and then turn right on Supai Highway. Continue 58 miles to the Hualapai Hilltop Trailhead at the end of the road. The Hualapai Trail is 8 miles to Supai Village.

From Kingman

Drive 58 miles east on AZ 66 (Andy Devine Avenue), passing through Peach Springs, and then turn left on Supai Highway. Continue 58 miles to the Hualapai Hilltop Trailhead at the end of the road. The Hualapai Trail is 8 miles to Supai Village.

Tip

This is a very remote area. Make sure you top off your fuel tank at Kingman, and carry extra water and food in your vehicle.

Grand Canyon West

From Kingman

Drive 44 miles north on Stockton Hill Road, and then turn right and drive 6.4 miles on Pierce Ferry Road. Turn right on Diamond Bar Road, and drive 16.6 miles. Bear left on Buck and Doe Road, and drive 4.5 miles to Grand Canyon West Airport.

Toroweap

From Kanab, Utah

Drive 7 miles south on US 89A. Turn right on Arizona 389. Drive 8.3 miles west, and then turn right on dirt County Road 109 (Mount Trumbull Road). After 37 miles, stay left on CR 5. Drive 6 miles, and then stay left on CR 115. Continue 14 miles, passing the Toroweap Ranger Station, to Toroweap Overlook and Campground. The section of road inside the park, from Toroweap Ranger Station to Toroweap Overlook, usually requires a high clearance vehicle.

> **Tip**
>
> This is another very remote area. Make sure you top off your fuel tank at Kanab or Fredonia, and carry extra water and food in your vehicle.

Grand Canyon-Parashant National Monument

The national monument is approximately 30 miles southwest of St. George, Utah. The main access is from St. George. Drive south on River Road 8 miles to the Utah/Arizona border. From here, several dirt roads provide access to points within the monument. All of the roads on the national monument are dirt and are impassable in wet weather.

Tip

There are no services or facilities in the national monument, so visitors must be prepared for desert back road driving and camping. Top off your fuel tank in St. George, and plan to carry all the water, food, and other supplies you'll need for your entire visit.

Park Entrance Fees

Grand Canyon National Park entrance permits and passes cover entrance fees to the national park only and do not cover campground fees. You can purchase an entrance permit, valid for seven days, or several different passes which are valid for one year or more. Permits and passes can be obtained at the park entrance stations, at ranger stations and visitor centers in the park, and at select businesses outside the park.

Some Grand Canyon destinations outside the national park and monument charge fees which are not covered by National Park passes. These destinations include Supai on the Havasupai Indian Reservation and Grand Canyon West on the Hualapai Indian Reservation.

See these websites for more information: www.havasupai-nsn.gov/tourism.html, www.grandcanyonwest.com.

Entry Permits and Passes

- Vehicle Permit: $30, admits one private vehicle and all its passengers for seven days

- Motorcycle Permit: $25, admits one private motorcycle and its passengers for seven days

- Individual Permit: $15, admits one person, arriving on foot or bicycle for seven days

- Grand Canyon National Park Annual Pass: $60, good for one year at Grand Canyon National Park only

- America the Beautiful Pass: $80, good for one year at all national parks, national monuments, and other federal recreation sites that charge entrance fees

- Senior Pass: $10, a lifetime pass to all federal lands charging an entrance fee, including national parks. Available to U.S. citizens or permanent residents age 62 and over

- Access Pass: Free, a lifetime pass to all federal lands charging an entrance fee, including national parks. Available to U.S. citizens or permanent residents with permanent disabilities

- Volunteer Pass: Free, valid for one year at all federal lands charging an entrance fee, including national parks. Available to volunteers who have done 500 hours of volunteer service on an annual basis

- Military Pass: Free for one year for active duty military personnel and dependents

Fees are subject to change- for current information, see the park website: http://www.nps.gov/grca/planyourvisit/fees.htm

Tip

The annual America the Beautiful Pass pays for itself very quickly if you visit several national parks or monuments in a year.

What To Do

As a hiker, climber, and photographer who's been exploring the Grand Canyon for decades, it's hard for me to imagine only having an hour or two at the Canyon. But that may be all the time you have. On the other hand, you may be lucky enough to have a week or two to devote to exploration. In any case, here's a list of suggestions of the best way to spend your time. Of course, there are many other options, but these are the ones I recommend.

A Couple of Hours

Rim Trail

During the winter off season, park at Bright Angel Lodge and walk the Rim Trail to the east (right) as far as you like. (During high season, from March through November, park at Maswik Lodge and take the free Park Shuttle to Bright Angel Lodge or El Tovar Hotel.) The Rim Trail offers classic views of the eastern Grand Canyon, and the view gets progressively better as you continue east. The trail passes historic Kolb and Lookout studios, as well as El Tovar Hotel and Hopi House. You can buy gift items at all of these places, and there are several places to eat, including the Arizona Room at Bright Angel Lodge and the restaurant at El Tovar.

If you continue past Verkamps Visitor Center, the Rim Trail becomes the Trail of Time. Along the trail, one meter represents one million years, as marked by brass caps set in the trail. The Trail of Time covers the entire geologic history of the Grand Canyon, from about 1.9 billion years ago to the present. Exhibits and samples of the Canyon's rock layers explain the geology as you walk. And after you pass Verkamps, there are no more facilities until you reach Yapapai Point, so the crowds thin out. The section of Rim Trail between Bright Angel Lodge and Yavapai Point, including the Trail of Time, is handicap-accessible.

AZ 64 Loop

Another option, for those who happen to be traveling on I-40 and US 89, is detouring through the park on AZ 64. From the north, when traveling south on US 89, turn right (west) on AZ 64 at Cameron, and proceed through the East Entrance station into the park. Then continue west on Desert View Drive along the South Rim. Then, at the junction with the South Entrance Road, turn left and leave the park on AZ 64 south. You'll pass though the gateway town of Tusayan just outside the park, where there are numerous places to eat, as well as gift shops. Continue south on AZ to I-40 at Williams. If you're traveling east on I-40 and then north on AZ 89, turn left (north) on AZ 64 at Williams to do this drive in reverse.

Tip

If you're driving Desert View Drive, stop at Lipan, Moran, and Grandview points for a series of excellent views of the changing and especially colorful geology at the eastern end of the Grand Canyon.

Half a Day

Hermits Rest

During the winter off season, drive the Hermit Road and take in the viewpoints along the way, especially Trail View, Mohave, Hopi, and Pima Points. During high season, from March through November, park at Maswick Lodge, take the free Village Shuttle to the Hermit Shuttle Transfer Point at Bright Angel Trailhead, then take Hermit Shuttle to Hermits Rest and back. The Rim Trail parallels the road, and the shuttle stops at most of the view points. Take advantage of this to walk part of the Rim Trail between viewpoints. Although there may be hundreds of people at the viewpoints, a short walk along the Rim Trail leaves the crowds behind.

Desert View Drive

You can also spend half a day driving Desert View Drive and checking out the viewpoints. From Tusayan, continue north into the park, then turn east (right) on Desert View Drive to Desert view. Return the same way. During the summer, you can have lunch at Desert View at the east end of the drive, or you can stop at Tusayan after leaving the park.

Hike to Cedar Ridge

If you really want to get a feel for the Grand Canyon, park at Grand Canyon Visitor Center (if the lot is full, continue to Maswick Lodge and take the free Village Shuttle to Grand Canyon Visitor Center.) Then take the free Kaibab Shuttle to the Kaibab Trailhead. Hike the South Kaibab Trail to Cedar Ridge and back to to the rim. This is a three-mile round-trip hike, and at Cedar Ridge you'll be about 1,000 feet below the South Rim, deep enough into the canyon to get a feel for its incredible scale. The South Kaibab Trail is on a ridge for much of its length, and offers much better views than the upper Bright Angel Trail.

Tip

Bring and drink plenty of water, especially during the hot summer months. Also, wear a broad-brimmed sun hat and use plenty of sunscreen.

A Full Day

Hermits Rest

Drive or take the Hermit Shuttle out to Hermits Rest and back, and then take a leisurely drive along Desert View Drive, as described above. Don't miss Trail View, Hopi, Mohave, and Pima points on the Hermit Road, and Grandview, Moran, and Lipan points on Desert View Drive. Once you leave the park and turn southbound on AZ 89 toward Flagstaff, turn left (east) off the highway south of Gray Mountain, and drive the

Wupatki-Sunset Crater Loop. This paved road takes you through Wupatki National Monument, where there are more than 100 pueblo-style prehistoric ruins. Be sure to stop at the Wupakti Visitor Center and take the short walk around Wupatki Ruin. Then continue through Sunset Crater Volcano National Monument. Stop at the base of Sunset Crater and take the Lava Flow Trail to learn more about this red-tinted volcano that erupted in 1066 AD. Then continue west to rejoin US 89 just north of Flagstaff.

North Rim

From Jacob Lake, drive south about 40 miles to North Rim Village. The North Rim gets a fraction of the visitation of the South Rim, and also offers a completely different perspective on the Canyon. Since the North Rim borders the high Kaibab Plateau, you'll travel through beautiful forest to reach the North Rim. Grand Canyon Lodge is located at the end of the road, and is one of the most unique of all American national park lodges. The dining room has a fine view of the Canyon. Walk the paved trail to Bright Angel Point by all means, but for a more intimate view of the Canyon, turn right instead of left at the lodge, and walk the Transept Trail above the deep gorge of The Transept. This trail brings home the fact that the Grand Canyon is really a complex of hundreds of side canyons, rather than a single canyon as it sometimes appears from the South Rim.

Tip

For total crowd avoidance, visit the North Rim between October 15 and November 15. The North Rim Campground, Grand Canyon Lodge, and all other facilities at North Rim Village close for the winter, but the roads to the viewpoints stay open until Novembers 15, or the first heavy snowfall.

Don't miss Point Imperial and Cape Royal, accessible via the Cape Royal Road just north of North Rim Village. Point Imperial is the highest point on either rim of the Canyon, at

8,800 feet. And it can be argued that Cape Royal is the best viewpoint on either rim that is accessible by paved road. The Canyon sweeps around this promontory for a 270-degree view. In the foreground, several of the Canyon's most impressive summits, inclduing Wotans Throne and Vishnu Temple, add depth to the view.

Several Days

If you have several days, you can do all the activities mentioned previously in this chapter, without feeling rushed at any point. With four or more days, spend a couple days on the South Rim and on the North Rim. You'll really get a feel for the scale and immensity of the Canyon when you look at it from both rims on the same trip.

Tip

Spend a few days at Grand Canyon, rather than trying to combine several national parks into one trip. Looking at a road map, it appears to be a short drive between the Canyon and Zion, Bryce, Capitol Reef, Canyonlands, and Arches national parks to the north in Utah. Trust me, it's not.

Sunrise and Sunset

If you're staying at a lodge inside the park, or in Tusayan, catch a sunset or a sunrise at the rim of the canyon. See the chapter "Photography Secrets" for tips on the best viewpoints.

Tip

Sunrise is less crowded than sunset, simply because most people who are on vacation don't want to get up early.

Hiking

On the South Rim, walk all of the Rim Trail from the South Kaibab Trailhead to Hermits Rest and watch how the Canyon evolves and changes along its length. Do one or more of the day hikes (see "Hiking and Backpacking") on the upper Hermit, South Kaibab, or Grandview Trails. On the North Rim, walk the Ken Patrick Trail for a cool walk through the magnificent North Rim forest. Or hike down the North Kaibab Trail to Roaring Springs and back.

Backpacking

If you're visiting during spring or fall, and you're fit and experienced, do one of the backpack trips in the "Hiking and Backpacking" chapter.

Tip

Although permits are required for overnight camping within the Canyon, and they are often reserved months in advance for popular trails and times, you can hang out at the Backcountry Information Center near Maswik Lodge before 9:00 am and try to pick up a cancellation for a same-day start to your hike.

Enjoying the View

By far the most popular activity at the Grand Canyon is enjoying the view from the many viewpoints. Hermit Road and Desert View Drive closely parallel the South Rim for a total of about 40 miles and provide access to a dozen or so major viewpoints and many more minor view points. While there are only three viewpoints on the North Rim that are accessible by paved road, these views make up for loss of quantity by providing probably the best views of all- at least, from a paved road.

> ### Tip
>
> The Grand Canyon's most spectacular rim viewpoints are reserved for those who have a high-clearance vehicle and are willing to leave the pavement or to walk a mile or so. But if you do so, you will leave the crowds behind, and may even have the rim to yourself.

The following viewpoint descriptions cover the paved South and North rim roads, then the back road viewpoints, and finally some very special viewpoints reserved for those willing to hike a bit.

South Rim

The South Rim viewpoints are in three groups- Grand Canyon Village viewpoints accessible from the free Village and Kaibab shuttles, the Hermit Road (accessible only by free shuttle except in the winter), and Desert View Drive (accessible only by car.)

Village Viewpoints

You can park your car almost anywhere in Grand Canyon Village and catch the free Village Shuttle, which runs in a loop through the entire village. While the obvious place to park is at the main shuttle transfer point at Grand Canyon Visitor

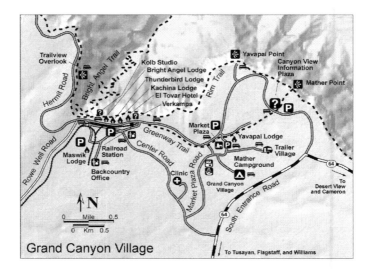

Center (see map), this parking lot is often full from March through November. In that case, head for the huge parking lot at Maswick Lodge, at the west end of the village. I'm going to assume you've parked at Maswick or Grand Canyon Visitor Center in the following description of the village viewpoints, but if you park elsewhere, just pick up the narrative at that place.

Grand Canyon Visitor Center

If you board the Village Shuttle at Maswick Lodge, the first stop of interest is Grand Canyon Visitor Center. Of course, if you managed to find a parking spot at the visitor center, you're already there. This complex includes the main park visitor center, where you can see a large relief map of the entire Grand Canyon, watch an informative movie on the Canyon, and ask questions at the information desk.

The park gift shop and bookstore, operated by the non-profit Grand Canyon Association, is also located in the plaza. In addition, there's a small cafe and a bicycle rental shop. Finally, the visitor center complex has the main shuttle transfer point, where you have a choice of the Village, Kaibab, and during the summer, the Tusayan shuttles.

Mather Point

Accessible via a quarter-mile trail from Grand Canyon Visitor Center or as the first stop on the Village Shuttle, Mather Point is the first view of the canyon for many visitors. The viewpoint itself is located at the tip of a spectacular fin of Kaibab limestone which projects out into the canyon. Mather Point is an excellent location for sunrise photos. Walk east along the paved Rim Trail to get a view of Mather Point itself and the sheer, sunlit cliffs below standing in sharp contrast to the early morning shadows of the canyon depths in the background.

To the east, you can see the upper portion of the South Kaibab Trail. The initial portion of the trail where it descends through the Kaibab limestone rim cliffs is hidden from view in a north facing alcove, but then the trail comes into view as it descends below Yaki Point along the sloping terrace eroded from the Toroweap formation. As the trail comes out onto the red slopes of the Hermit shale, it swings around the east side of O'Neill Butte and disappears from view.

Pipe Creek is visible below as well as a portion of the 72-mile long Tonto Trail winding along the greenish-gray shale slopes of the Tonto Plateau. This section of the Tonto Trail is in better shape and more visible from above because it has been used several times as part of the main rim to river route on the Bright Angel Trail. The original route of the Bright Angel Trail was down upper Garden Creek, along the Tonto Plateau across Pipe Creek, and then down to the Colorado River along what is now the lower South Kaibab Trail. After the River Trail was completed to connect lower Pipe Creek to the two footbridges across the Colorado River at the mouth of Bright Angel Creek and the foot of the Kaibab Trail, the Tonto Trail fell into disuse except by backcountry hikers. It was temporarily used as the main route again when the lower Bright Angel Trail in Pipe Creek was closed for reconstruction for several years.

The Plateau Point Trail is also visible leaving the green, spring-fed oasis of Indian Garden and heading out to a viewpoint just west of Garden Creek. Plateau Point is unusually flat for the Tonto plateau and part of the trail crosses a landing strip used by RV Thomas and Ellsworth Kolb to land a plane and take off again, on August 8, 1922. Emory Kolb hiked down to the airstrip to photograph the event.

To the north, on the far side of Granite Gorge, you'll note Bright Angel Canyon. Phantom Ranch, the only resort at the bottom of the Grand Canyon, and Bright Angel Campground are located at the mouth of Bright Angel Creek just above the Colorado River on the North Kaibab Trail. The trail continues most of the way up Bright Angel Creek before climbing up Roaring Springs Canyon to North Rim Village.

Yaki Point

From the shuttle transfer point at Grand Canyon Visitor Center use the Kaibab Trail Shuttle to reach this viewpoint overlooking the Kaibab Trail descending past red O'Neill Butte. Since private cars are not allowed, Yaki Point is a relatively quiet place to watch the sunrise or sunset.

The view includes much of the upper South Kaibab Trail. Some visitors wonder why this popular trail was located four miles east of Grand Canyon Village. The answer is that it was built by the Park Service as an alternate route to the Bright Angel Trail, which was under private ownership in 1919 and not accessible to the public when the national park was created.

O'Neill Butte is a major landmark along the Kaibab Trail. The red cliffs of the butte are carved from the upper sandstone layers of the Supai formation. The butte is named after Bucky O'Neill, a member of Theodore Roosevelt's Rough Riders.

Cremation Canyon lies to the east of the Kaibab Trail and is one of the sites where the famous split-twig figurines of the Grand Canyon have been discovered. These ancient artifacts were made from a single twig split down the middle and folded into animal shapes. Willow was most often used due to the wood's flexibility. Dating from 2,000 to 4,000 years old, split-twig figurines are found in remote, undisturbed caves where they are protected from the weather. You can see some examples of these remarkable artifacts at the Tusayan Museum on Desert View Drive.

Yavapai Point

After Mather Point, the next stop on the Kaibab Shuttle is Yavapai Point. You can drive here, but the parking lot is often full from March through November. You can also reach Yavapai Point via the Rim Trail from Mather Point or El Tovar Hotel.

Yavapai Point features views of Bright Angel Creek to the north and Pipe Creek to the east. Look for the patch of cottonwood trees and buildings along Garden Creek marking the ranger station and campground at Indian Garden along the Bright Angel Trail. A small museum and book store, Yavapai Observation Station offers exhibits explaining the fascinating geology of the Grand Canyon. This point is also the end of the Trail of Time, which starts near Verkamps and explains the geologic history and rock formations of the Canyon through time markers and exhibits.

Yavapai Point features a web cam and is an air quality monitoring station for the park. Visitors to national parks expect to see clear, unpolluted air, but unfortunately national parks do not exist under a sealed dome. They are part of the regional environment, which in the Southwest includes such nearby pollution sources as coal-fired power plants in the Four Corners area, various mining operations, and the large metropolitan areas of Phoenix, Las Vegas, and Los Angeles.

Part of the purpose of the national park air monitoring program is to determine the source of pollutants by studying the pollution particles in the air. The nature of the particles identifies the source, and this information is used by government agencies and private enterprise to reduce the amount of pollutants at their sources.

Within the park, the Park Service reduces pollution by operating an alternative fuel vehicle fleet for administrative purposes. The park also operates a free year-round shuttle bus system throughout the Grand Canyon Village area, and to the Kaibab Trailhead and Yaki Point. Except in the winter, free shuttles also run along the Hermit Road and to Tusayan.

El Tovar Hotel

While not a named viewpoint, the view of Garden Creek and the upper Bright Angel Trail from the rim in front of the historic hotel is classic- and very crowded from March through November. But for a real treat, walk this section of the Rim Trail from El Tovar to Bright Angel Trailhead during the winter. The light on the canyon walls is much softer than during the summer months, and snow on the upper terraces highlights the colors of the rock layers. Plus, you can often

---

Tip

Hermit Road makes a great scenic drive when it is open to private cars during the winter. Otherwise, you must ride the free Hermit Shuttle to get to the viewpoints and this portion of the Rim Trail.

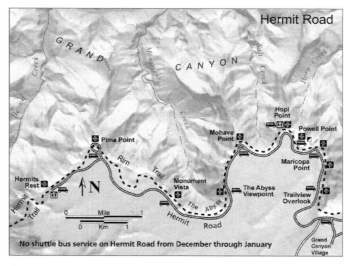

No shuttle bus service on Hermit Road from December through January

walk right into the restaurant at El Tovar and even get one of their few tables with a view of the Canyon.

Hermit Road

The Hermit Road and the mileage log start at the west end of Grand Canyon Village and follows the canyon rim to the west for 7 miles. The road ends at Hermits Rest and the Hermit Trailhead. The Rim Trail also follows the rim out to Hermits Rest.

0.0 Hermit/Village Shuttle Transfer Stop

Private cars are not allowed on the Hermit Road except during the winter. The shuttle is a great way to travel the Hermit Road because it stops at all the major viewpoints. You can spend as much time at the viewpoints as you wish and catch the shuttle to the next one, or walk the Rim Trail between shuttle stops. The mileage log starts at the Hermit Shuttle Stop, located at the Bright Angel Trailhead at the west end of Grand Canyon Village. The Village Shuttle also stops here, allowing you to transfer between shuttles.

Another great way to enjoy the Hermit Road is by bicycle during spring, summer and fall when the free shuttle is operating. Because private cars are not allowed except during the winter, riding the Hermit Road is a quiet and relaxing experience. The shuttle buses have bicycle racks, so you can ride the Hermit Road one way and take the shuttle the other. The best way to do this is to take the shuttle to Hermits Rest and ride back to Grand Canyon Village, which avoids the climb from the Hermit/Village Shuttle Stop.

Before boarding the shuttle, have a look off the rim. You are standing at the head of Garden Creek, the canyon containing the Bright Angel Trail. You are also standing on the Bright Angel Fault. The rim to your left has been raised about 180 feet higher than the rim beneath your feet. The resulting fracture weakened the rocks and allowed water to carve out the canyon below you. The fault also broke down the Redwall limestone cliff at the head of Garden Creek and created a route that native Americans used to descend the canyon. The same break was used when the modern Bright Angel Trail was constructed. The Bright Angel Fault continues southwest across the Coconino Plateau behind you, and also to the northeast across the Grand Canyon onto the North Rim. Bright Angel Canyon follows the Bright Angel Fault north of the Colorado River, and the North Kaibab Trail in turn follows Bright Angel Canyon.

1.2 Trailview Overlook

Trailview Overlook looks to the east over upper Garden Creek and Grand Canyon Village. You are seemingly looking straight down on the Bright Angel Trail as it switchbacks down the break in the cliffs caused by the Bright Angel Fault. Most Grand Canyon trails and routes take advantage of such fault breaks.

The Redwall limestone is an especially formidable obstacle. This massive limestone formation is about halfway between rim and river and persists throughout the length of the Grand Canyon. The Redwall limestone forms about 1,000 miles of cliffs that are uniformly about 550 feet high throughout the Canyon. Along the length of the Grand Canyon there are only about 200 known breaks where the Redwall limestone can be descended without technical climbing gear. Although most of these breaks are mainly used by wildlife and the occasional backcountry hiker, all of the Grand Canyon's trails except for the North and South Kaibab use natural fault breaks in the Redwall limestone.

1.7 Maricopa Point

Maricopa Point overlooks the inactive Orphan Lode Mine, operated from 1891 to 1967. Originally a copper mine, the Orphan Lode began exploiting uranium deposits in the 1950s. Although the park now owns the mine, environmental cleanup has been difficult, which highlights the hazards associated with uranium mining in the region.

The Battleship, a distinctive butte in the reddish Supai formation, is prominent below to the northeast. For many years, employees of the Fred Harvey Company, which operated the hotels and concessions on the South Rim, would climb The Battleship on the Fourth of July and replace the

American flag that flew on the summit. As Grand Canyon summits go, the Battleship is an easy climb. It can be reached from the Bright Angel Trail and a short cross-country hike along the terraces in the Supai formation. Easy rock scrambling leads to the summit. Still, it is not a hike for the inexperienced. Stick to the Bright Angel and Kaibab trails for your first hike into the canyon.

2.2 Powell Point

Powell Point commemorates the two historic voyages of exploration down the Colorado River through the Grand Canyon undertaken by Major John Wesley Powell and his boat crews in 1869 and 1871. Major Powell named the Grand Canyon and was the first to explore and map the region. Before Powell's first voyage, the Grand Canyon region was marked "unexplored" on maps. Many predicted that Powell's voyage would end in disaster because the Colorado River would go over a waterfall that could not be portaged or run, and the expedition would be trapped in a canyon that could not be climbed.

Powell, as a trained geologist, was certain that there would be no waterfalls in the canyons of the Green and Colorado Rivers that he proposed to run. Waterfalls are very young landscape features (for example, Niagara Falls is less than 10,000 years old) and Powell knew that the Grand Canyon is millions of years old. He did assume that there would be ferocious rapids along the river, so he ordered strong oak boats. Although his boats didn't turn out to be the best river craft, they did the job. Powell and his men ran the river system from Green River, Wyoming, without any serious injuries or loss of life.

Powell brought along a photographer and an artist, so his expeditions not only produced the first detailed maps of the region, but also the first images of the Grand Canyon of the Colorado River, as he named the canyon.

2.4 Hopi Point

Hopi Point is a good place to catch the sunset glow on the canyon walls to the north and east and also offers views of the Colorado River. Dana Butte forms the end of the Redwall limestone point almost directly to the north. There are restrooms at Hopi Point.

The view from Hopi Point is the classic eastern Grand Canyon panorama. The upper two-thirds of the canyon is a sequence of cliffs formed in the hard Kaibab limestone, Supai formation, and Redwall limestone. Narrow terraces between the cliffs are formed on the softer rocks of the Toroweap formation, Hermit shale, and shale layers in the Supai formation.

About 3,500 feet below the rim, a major terrace forms on the Bright Angel shale. This shale layer is much thicker than the shale layers above and below, so the soft rock erodes easily and undermines the Muav and Redwall limestone cliffs above. The cliffs recede to form a wide terrace known as the Tonto Plateau. This plateau is about 1,200 feet above the Colorado River and is the dominant terrace in the eastern third of the Grand Canyon, which is the portion visible from the Hermit Road.

3.1 Mohave Point

Mohave Point is a good spot for canyon sunrises, as it looks north and west at rock faces lit by the rising sun. It also offers views of the Tonto Plateau, Granite Gorge, and the Colorado River.

While most of the trails in the Grand Canyon descend from rim to river, several trails traverse the terraces in the canyon. The best known such trail is the Tonto Trail, which winds along the Tonto Plateau from Red Canyon on the east to Garnet Canyon on the west, a distance of 72 miles. The trail was originally built by prospectors but very little of the trail was actually constructed. Most of the trail was created from the repeated passage of miners and their pack animals. Some construction was done where the trail crossed side canyons. When prospecting ceased in the Grand Canyon after the creation of the national park, the Tonto Trail fell into disuse and was maintained mostly by wild burros, the feral descendants of the prospector's pack stock.

As you can see by looking down on the Tonto Plateau from Mohave Point, the Tonto Trail is anything but straight. The trail is constantly detouring around the heads of side canyons and side canyons of side canyons as well as every little ravine. It spends some of its time out on the very edge of the gorge containing the Colorado River, but much of the time the Tonto Trail is back in the recesses of the canyons. Not so apparent from the rim viewpoints is the fact that the Tonto Plateau is anything but level. It only appears flat from above because of the extreme terrain above and below. While hiking the Tonto Trail you are constantly climbing and descending and winding around side canyons. It's definitely an exercise in patience. The best thing to do is take your time and enjoy the ever-changing views.

3.7 The Abyss

At The Abyss, the shale layers that normally form terraces between the upper cliffs are unusually thin, so the cliffs form a nearly sheer wall below the South Rim at the head of Monument Creek. This is a vivid example of how small variations in the rock layers can create major differences in the topography of the Grand Canyon. In fact, the upper cliffs of the Grand Canyon are so persistent and have so few breaks along the Hermit Road that there are no known routes from the rim to the Colorado River between the Bright Angel and Hermit trails.

5.2 Monument Creek Vista

Overlooking the headwaters of Monument Creek, this viewpoint and shuttle stop is also the trailhead for the Greenway Trail, a handicap-accessible trail following the old 1912 alignment of Hermit Road. Monument Creek features a permanent stream and has created a ferocious rapid where it meets the Colorado River.

Contrary to popular impressions, rapids along the Colorado River in the Grand Canyon are not the remnants of old waterfalls. Instead, every Grand Canyon rapid forms where debris has been washed down a side canyon into the river. When a heavy thundershower or prolonged rain falls into a side canyon, the resulting runoff quickly gathers speed as it descends the steep slopes of bare rock and sparsely vegetated soil. The ability of flowing water to carry sand, pebbles, cobbles, and boulders increases rapidly with the water's speed, enabling the flooding side canyon to carry large amounts of debris to the river. This debris forms a partial dam in the river. The river ponds up behind the dam and then gains speed over the submerged rocks, creating a rapid. Because the river flows much more slowly than the side canyon floods, it takes hundreds of years to wear away the boulders that created the rapid.

6.2 Pima Point

Pima Point looks down on Hermit Camp, the site of a major tourist camp operated on the edge of Hermit Creek on the Tonto Plateau. An aerial tramway once spanned the 4,000-foot space between Pima Point and Hermit Camp and was used to haul supplies to and from the site.

When Grand Canyon National Park was created in 1919, the present Grand Canyon Village was already the focus of tourist activity on the South Rim due to the arrival of the Santa Fe Railroad a few years before. The only problem was that there wasn't a freely accessible trail to the Colorado River. The Bright Angel Trail was still privately owned, and the owner charged an exorbitant fee for the use of his trail. Fred Harvey Company wanted to build a tourist camp below the rim, so they built the Hermit Road out to to the head of Hermit Canyon west of Grand Canyon Village, and then built the Hermit Trail down Hermit Creek to the Colorado River.

Hermit Camp was established on the Tonto Plateau just east of Hermit Creek. Tent cabins accommodated guests, and the camp was complete with running water and even a Model T Ford that was sent down in pieces on the aerial tramway. Hermit Trail continued to the river along lower Hermit Creek, though little of the original construction has survived the periodic floods.

When the National Park Service gave up on buying the Bright Angel Trail and constructed the South Kaibab Trail as an alternate route to the river below Grand Canyon Village in the late 1920's, Fred Harvey Company opened a new tourist camp, Phantom Ranch, along lower Bright Angel Creek. When the North Kaibab Trail was completed, creating a trail across the Grand Canyon from Grand Canyon Village to North Rim Village, Phantom Ranch took over from Hermit Camp as the premier tourist camp within the canyon, and Hermit Camp was abandoned.

7.0 Hermits Rest

Hermit Road ends here, at the small gift shop and snack bar occupying the historic building designed by famed Grand Canyon architect Mary Colter. Hermits Rest is also the trailhead for the Hermit Trail, originally built to access Hermit Creek. The Dripping Springs Trail connects the upper Hermit Trail to the upper Boucher Trail, and together with a segment of the Tonto Trail forms a loop hike very popular with backpackers. A rewarding day hike can be made down the upper Hermit Trail to Santa Maria Spring. The spring is not reliable but the view is.

Desert View Drive

Desert View Drive starts from the South Rim Entrance Road just east of Grand Canyon Visitor Center and north of Tusayan. You can leave the park at Desert View and continue east on AZ 64 to reach US 89, the main north-south highway across northern Arizona.

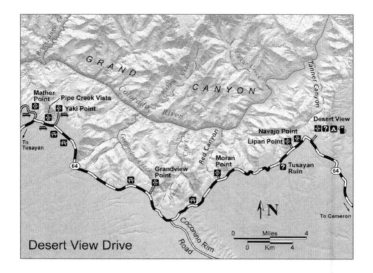

Desert View Drive

0.0 Intersection of South Rim and Desert View Drives

Desert View Drive and the mileage log start at the T-intersection on the South Rim Entrance Road, east of Grand Canyon Visitor Center and follows the South Rim 21 miles east to Desert View. In addition to the named viewpoints, there are several unnamed viewpoints and quiet picnic areas along the road.

0.7 Pipe Creek Vista

This viewpoint is on the left next to the road and can be reached by car or the free Kaibab Shuttle. Pick up the Kaibab Shuttle at the Grand Canyon Visitor Center. It is the first viewpoint after entering Desert View Drive from the South Rim Entrance Road. From here, you're looking down Pipe Creek. A section of the Tonto Trail is visible snaking along the Tonto Plateau about 3,000 feet below the rim. The original Bright Angel Trail used this section of the Tonto Trail as part of its route from rim to river. The Rim Trail runs along the South Rim From Hermits Rest to the South Kaibab Trailhead.

There are shuttle bus stops at the major viewpoints along the Rim Trail, which lets you walk any part and then catch the shuttle.

1.2 Yaki Point and Kaibab Trailhead

The side road to Yaki Point and the South Kaibab Trailhead is accessible only via the Kaibab Trail Shuttle. Yaki Point offers a view of the upper South Kaibab Trail. This trail was built by the Park Service during the 1920's shortly after the creation of the national park to avoid tolls on the privately-owned Bright Angel Trail. Together with the North Kaibab Trail, the trail is the only maintained trail across the Grand Canyon from the South Rim to the North Rim. But the Kaibab Trail wasn't the first trans-canyon trail. That honor goes to the South and North Bass trails, built by William Bass to reach his prospects and mine workings in the Bass Canyon and Shinumo Creek areas, far to the west of the Kaibab Trail. Like several other miners, Bass later used his trails to guide tourists. By ferrying his customers across the Colorado River in a boat or taking them across on a cableway, he could guide them from the South Rim to the North Rim and back.

8.8 Grandview Point

Well-named Grandview Point is not only the trailhead for the Grandview Trail but also one of the best viewpoints on the South Rim. The panoramic views overlook Horseshoe Mesa, Hance Canyon, and the Colorado River. This area was also the location of the first hotel at the rim of the Grand Canyon. Grandview Hotel was a log structure located southeast of Grandview Point along the rim. It was the primary destination for early visitors who arrived by stagecoach from Flagstaff or Williams. Grandview Hotel's only competition was from tent camps on the rim to the east and west. Once the railroad reached Grand Canyon Village in 1901 and El Tovar Hotel was completed in 1905, the Village area became the focus of tourism on the South Rim and Grandview Hotel was abandoned. Today little remains to mark the site except a few pieces of crockery.

14.6 Moran Point

At Moran Point, you can clearly see the transition in the canyon's geology as the soft, colorful, tilted rocks of the Grand Canyon Supergroup, which make up the floor of the canyon to the east, give way to the hard, dark gray rocks of the Vishnu Schist, which forms Granite Gorge to the west.

The Grand Canyon Supergroup is not present throughout the Grand Canyon. These layers of rock were deposited on top of the Vishnu schist and then uplifted and faulted to form a major mountain range. Most of those mountains, and the Supergroup, were eroded away before the Tapeats sandstone was deposited on top of the Vishnu schist.

18.5 Tusayan Museum

Located off the south side of Desert View Drive between Moran and Lipan points, this small museum has exhibits and books that explain the nearby ruin from the Pueblo period. An easy trail loops around the ruin and there are restrooms and a small picnic area.

19.7 Lipan Point

Located on a promontory projecting out over the canyon, Lipan Point has fine views of the colorful geology of the eastern canyon. The floor of the canyon to the northeast is dominated by the soft, colorful shales and sandstones of the Grand Canyon Supergroup, a tilted layer of ancient rocks which is best exposed at the eastern end of the Grand Canyon. The Colorado River meanders through this landscape as it passes Tanner and Unkar rapids. Lipan Point is also the trailhead for the Tanner Trail, a steep, unmaintained trail which descends past Escalante and Cardenas buttes to Tanner Rapids at the Colorado River.

20.8 Navajo Point

Navajo Point looks down on Escalante and Cardenas buttes and also offers a view of the Tanner Trail winding along the base of the buttes. Escalante Butte and nearby Escalante Creek were named for Francisco Escalante, a Spanish missionary who was a member of the Dominguez party. The Dominguez expedition attempted to find an overland route from Santa Fe to Monterrey on the California coast in 1776.

Cardenas Butte and nearby Cardenas Creek are named after Lieutenant Lopez de Cardenas, a member of the Coronado Expedition which traveled north from Mexico City and eventually along the present Arizona-New Mexico border. Cardenas was detached from the main expedition and sent west to confirm reports of a great river. With the assistance of Hopi guides, Cardenas reached the South Rim somewhere between Desert View and Moran Point in 1542.

21.4 Desert View

Located at the east end of Desert View Drive, Desert View features the Watchtower, a structure designed by Mary Colter and inspired by the ruins of watchtowers used by prehistoric inhabitants of the canyon country. The tower and the viewpoint below it will both give you stunning views of the eastern canyon, including the especially sheer cliffs of the Palisades of the Desert and the Desert Facade.

Services at Desert View include a gift shop, snack bar, bookstore, information center, service station, campground, and restrooms. The East Entrance Station is also located at Desert View.

North Rim

The view from the North Rim is quite different from that of the South Rim. Because side canyons that drain into the Colorado River from the north drain the Kaibab Plateau as well, they are much longer than their South Rim counterparts. The river is much closer to the South Rim than the north, and most of the canyon's mesas, buttes, temples, and connecting ridge lines are north of the river. Summits that tend to blend in as seen from the South Rim stand out in strong relief when seen from the North Rim.

The roads to the North Rim viewpoints travel through beautiful, mixed conifer forest which is plenty of compensation for the lack of rim drives. There are also fewer viewpoints accessible by road but all of the North Rim viewpoints have unique and stunning views.

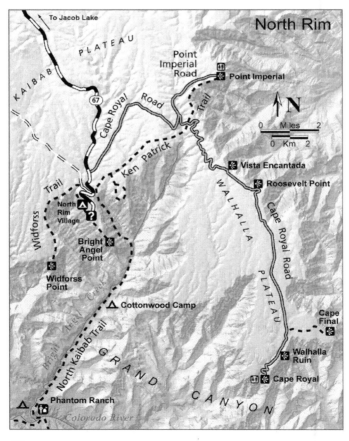

Bright Angel Point

The most popular viewpoint, Bright Angel Point, is reached from the main North Rim parking lot at the end of the North Rim Road either by walking through Grand Canyon Lodge and exiting from the veranda on the left, or by skirting the lodge cabins on the left. If you walk through the lodge, you'll see why this historic park lodge is justifiably famous. Since the lodge is built in a U-shape facing the parking area, it hides the view of the canyon until you go through the main entrance and see the canyon framed by the panoramic windows of the veranda at the foot of a flight of stairs. Although perched right on the edge of the canyon, Grand Canyon Lodge is built of native stone and blends in to the natural surroundings.

Whichever way you reach it, the paved trail continues about a quarter-mile along a narrow ridge to Bright Angel Point. There are a few stairs along the way. The viewpoint is within Bright Angel Canyon, a typical, long north-side canyon, so the views are more confined than other viewpoints. On the other hand, the depths of Roaring Springs Canyon are right below you, and on a quiet day you can hear Roaring Springs itself.

Cape Royal Scenic Drive

The Cape Royal Road is the North Rim's only paved access to rim viewpoints, but it is spectacular. It is a 23-mile one-way drive from Grand Canyon Lodge, and the suggested side trip to Point Imperial adds another 6.0 miles, for a total of 29 miles. The road passes through a beautiful mixed forest of Douglas and white firs, quaking aspen, and ponderosa pine. During the fall, the aspen lights up the forest in vibrant shades of yellow, orange, and red. The following mileage log starts from the North Rim Village parking lot at Grand Canyon Lodge and assumes you will take the side road to Point Imperial.

0.0 Grand Canyon Lodge

From the parking lot, drive north on the North Rim Road, passing North Rim Village with its campground, gas station, and general store on the left.

2.1 North Kaibab Trailhead

The only maintained trail across the Grand Canyon starts from this trailhead on the right. The North Kaibab Trail descends into Roaring Spring Canyon, and then follows Bright Angel Creek to the Colorado River, passing two backcountry campgrounds on the way. Phantom Ranch is located near the river, where hikers and mule riders can buy lunch and snacks, as well as spend the night.

3.0 Cape Royal Road

Turn right onto the Cape Royal Road (go straight ahead to exit the park.)

8.4 Point Imperial Road on the left

Point Imperial is a 3.0-mile side trip from the Cape Royal Road, which will add 6.0 miles to your drive. The mileages assume that you make this side trip, which is highly recommended.

11.4 Point Imperial

Point Imperial is the highest point on the North Rim at 8,800 feet. Here, on this lofty perch, you have a close view of Mount Hayden and a panoramic view of the complex of canyons formed by Nankoweap Creek. Nankoweap Creek has five major arms and a permanent stream in the main canyon. Hidden at the head of one of the arms is Goldwater Natural Bridge, which was discovered, lost, and then discovered again from the air by Senator Barry Goldwater. In the distance to the east and southeast, you are looking at the East Rim, which is about 3,000 feet lower than Point Imperial. The rimrock is the same on both rims- the Kaibab limestone. The reason for the difference in elevation is the East Kaibab Monocline. A monocline is a bend in the layers of rocks formed by uplift. In this case, the Kaibab Plateau, where you are standing, was uplifted 3,000 feet higher than the plateau to the east. Sometimes the rocks break along vertical fault lines, but in this case the rocks were deeply buried. Under high heat and pressure, the rocks were soft enough to bend instead of breaking. The East Kaibab Monocline is the longest exposed monocline in the world

14.4 Return to Cape Royal Road

Turn left to continue the scenic drive along the Cape Royal Road.

19.0 Vista Encantada

Vista Encantada (Spanish for Enchanted View) is a small pullout on the left with picnic tables. Fir trees frame a gorgeous view of Brady Butte above the headwaters of Nankoweap Creek. It's a quiet place to have a picnic lunch and enjoy the Canyon and the rim forest. Looking to the northeast, you can see the tilted rock layers exposed on the south side of Saddle Mountain and Boundary Ridge, which form the north end of the Grand Canyon. The tilted rock layers are the result of folding along the East Kaibab Monocline.

20.6 Roosevelt Point

Roosevelt Point, a small, quiet pullout on the left, offers a view into the south arm of Nankoweap Creek as well as views across the East Rim and the Navajo Indian Reservation in the distance. Picnic tables near the parking area are a good place to take a break. An easy 0.1 mile one-way trail offers a nice, cool stroll through the North Rim forest.

26.2 Cape Final Trail

A signed trailhead marks the start of the Cape Final Trail, which leads 2.0 miles one-way to Cape Final, an east-facing promontory towering high above the headwaters of Unkar Creek. Cape Final also offers close-up views of Jupiter and Juno temples, many other Grand Canyon summits, and part of the Painted Desert and Navajo Indian Reservations in the distance to the southeast.

27.2 Walhalla Ruin

Walhalla Overlook is on the left at a large parking lot. Across the road from the viewpoint, an interpretive trail loops around a small Indian ruin. The viewpoint overlooks Unkar Creek and Unkar Delta, where the creek meets the Colorado River. An extensive pre-Columbian ruin covers the delta. Archaeological evidence shows that the inhabitants of the Unkar Delta village and the Wahalla ruin routinely traveled back and forth from rim to river, hunting in the rim forest and farming the delta with water from the Colorado River. At least one modern tribe, the Havasupai, continue this practice today, farming at Supai Village in Havasu Canyon, and raising cattle instead of hunting on the South Rim. When the first European explorers reached the Grand Canyon, the Havasupai were also farming small plots at Indian Garden on the present Bright Angel Trail.

28.1 Cliff Springs Trail

The Cliff Springs Trail starts from a small pullout on the right. It is a 0.5-mile one way trail to a rare North Rim spring. Do not drink the water without purifying it. The reason that springs and surface water are so rare on the Kaibab Plateau despite the heavy winter snowfall is the layer of porous Kaibab limestone that forms the surface of the plateau. Meltwater and rainwater promptly soak into the ground, so that there are only a few springs and shallow lakes and no permanent streams. Additional porous layers below the Kaibab limestone let groundwater continue deep into the earth, until it encounters a layer of shale below the Redwall limestone that slows the downward percolation. The Redwall limestone is riddled with caverns dissolved out of the rock by the underground water, and some of this water finds outlets to the surface deep within the Grand Canyon. The resulting springs and permanent streams are a delight in the desert environment of the canyon.

28.7 Cape Royal

The road ends in the Cape Royal parking lot. From here it is an easy, level 0.25-mile walk to Cape Royal. This viewpoint is located at the southern tip of the Walhalla Plateau and has a 270-degree view of the eastern Grand Canyon. It is arguably the best Grand Canyon viewpoint that is accessible by paved road. Wotans Throne and Vishnu Temple, two of the most impressive of the canyon's many buttes and temples, dominate the foreground. A side trail leads out to the Angels Window overlook, which offers a view to the east at the verge of a 1,000-foot drop. Angels Window itself is a natural arch in the fin under the viewpoint.

Summits in the Grand Canyon are mountains in their own right. If Vishnu Temple was sliced off at its base and placed on the plateau, it would rise 5,000 feet above its base. Because most Grand Canyon summits are difficult to reach, requiring hours or days of strenuous cross-country hiking, the last summits weren't climbed until the 1980's. Few rock climbers are willing to carry heavy loads of climbing and camping gear over such rough terrain to reach climbs that are on soft, dangerous rock. Even Vishnu Temple, which was first climbed in 1933 by Merrel Clubb, had only 14 ascents by 1985. Although not difficult by rock climbing standards, climbing Vishnu Temple from the North Rim is a difficult two-day hike and scramble and the ascent of the peak requires great care.

Rim Walks

Maps

To keep the size and price of this book down, I haven't included maps of the hikes, but each hike includes a link to an online map. If you're reading the paperback edition of this book, just enter the short links into your phone or tablet to see the maps. Even better, if you have the ebook edition of this book on your phone or tablet, you can just click on the link directly to see the maps.

> ### Tip
>
> Here's the best tip in this book for avoiding crowds- walk. Most visitors to the Grand Canyon never venture more than a few feet from their car or a shuttle stop. Yet there are easy trails on both rims that nearly anyone can walk, at least for a short distance. And the South Rim has the handicap accessible Trail of Time, one of the best ways to get a feel for the vast sweep of time represented by the rocks in the Grand Canyon. I'm not promising total solitude on the rim trails, but you certainly won't have the crowds that the major view points experience.

South Rim

Rim Trail

The Rim Trail follows the South Rim for nearly 13 miles from Hermits Rest to South Kaibab Trailhead. It is an excellent trail for beginners or non-hikers, as elevation changes are limited to 300 feet, and the Village, Hermit, and Kaibab Trail shuttles stop at all the major viewpoints along the trail. You can walk between shuttle stops and make the hike as long or short as you want. The section between Bright Angel Lodge and Yavapai Point is handicap-accessible. The Trail of Time encompasses the paved section of the Rim Trail between

Verkamps Visitor Center and the Yavapai Point Geology Museum, a distance of 1.4 miles. Along the trail, each meter of distance represents a period of one million years, starting from the oldest rocks in the Grand Canyon at just under 1.9 billion years ago, to the present. Brass markers in the trail give the years before the present, and there are exhibits with samples of all the major Grand Canyon rock layers along the way, as well as informative signs. As it nears the Yavapai Point Museum, the trail transitions to a human time scale.

You can view an online trail map here: http://bit.ly/1Sz9aQv

> ### Tip
>
> I know I've said it before, but I'm going to say it again anyway- during warm weather, be sure to bring plenty of water- and drink it. Your body dehydrates quickly in the dry, high-altitude air, and dehydration can quickly lead to serious illness. Wear a sun hat and sun screen.

North Rim

Transept Trail

The Transept Trail follows the rim of Transept Canyon from Grand Canyon Lodge to North Rim Campground, a distance of 1.4 miles one-way. The trail is nearly level and gives you stunning views of The Transept, a deep tributary canyon of Bright Angel Creek.

You can view an online trail map here: http://bit.ly/226Rix2

Widforss Trail

The Widforss Trail starts from a trailhead across the road from the North Kaibab Trailhead, and winds 4.4 miles along the west rim of The Transept to a point on the North Rim overlooking Widforss Point.

You can view an online trail map here:
http://bit.ly/1ovWsWd

Uncle Jim Trail

This 2.5-mile trail starts at the North Kaibab Trailhead and traverses the forest to a viewpoint overlooking Roaring Springs Canyon and the Kaibab Trail.

You can view an online trail map here:
http://bit.ly/1SMrFza

Cape Final Trail

This trail starts from the Cape Final Trailhead along the Cape Royal Road and follows an old fire road 2.0 miles through the rim forest to Cape Final, a major promontory with excellent views of the eastern Grand Canyon.

You can view an online trail map here: http://bit.ly/1qqjShf

Back Roads

Although exploring the back roads of the park and surrounding national forest and other public lands is extremely rewarding, you must be prepared. You should have a high clearance vehicle (though four-wheel-drive is nice to have, it's not essential), and be prepared to be self-sufficient by carrying extra food, water, and clothing. During the summer, water is by far the most important item to have in your vehicle. It's safest to travel in convoys of two or more vehicles in case of breakdown. If you explore in a single vehicle, you must be prepared and equipped to walk out to the nearest paved road for help. Consider buying a Personal Locator Beacon, which works anywhere (except in narrow slot canyons) and can pinpoint your location to rescuers and summon help via satellite in case of a life-threatening emergency.

There are hundreds of miles of back roads on the plateaus surrounding the Canyon, enough for a lifetime of adventures. The following are just a few suggestions.

Havasupai Point

Accessible via the Rowe Well Road, which starts from the Hermit Shuttle Transfer Point at the west end of Grand Canyon Village, this long dirt road leads about 30 miles west to the South Bass Trailhead just west of Havasupai Point. A portion of this road passes through the Havasupai Indian Reservation, and the tribe may charge an access fee to cross their land. The last portion of the road, inside the national park, is unmaintained. You must have a high clearance vehicle to reach the rim, and this section of the road is often impassible during winter and spring due to snow and mud.

Tip

Do NOT depend on a cell phone to get help. There is very little cell phone coverage in the Grand Canyon backcountry.

But wow! The view from the South Bass Trailhead is stunning. Here, the geology of the Canyon undergoes a major change. The thick layer of Bright Angel Shale that creates the broad Tonto Plateau in the eastern Grand Canyon thins out to the west, and in this area this greenish-purplish-gray plateau, located about 3,500 feet below the rim, has already become much narrower and sloping. At the same time, the bright red Hermit Shale has become much thicker, creating a new, broad terrace at the base of the Coconino Sandstone. This terrace, known as the Esplanade, is located about 1,000 to 2,000 feet below the rim, and becomes much wider to the west of the South Bass Trail.

The South Bass Trail is named for William Wallace Bass, who along with his wife built the trail and established camps on the rim and down at the Colorado River to support his mining operations in the late nineteenth century. Like other miners from this period, he soon turned to guiding tourists. Bass built a cable tramway across the river and the North Bass Trail, the first trail to the North Rim, so that he could guide his clients all the way across the Canyon.

Point Sublime

Lying on the North Rim well to the west of North Rim Village, Point Sublime was named by Major John Wesley Powell after he was guided to this point in 1870. Best known for his two historic runs of the Colorado River through the Grand Canyon, Major Powell and his Powell Survey also explored the Colorado Plateau. Point Sublime is without a doubt the most stunning Grand Canyon rim viewpoint on either rim.

The Point Sublime Road starts from the North Rim Entrance Road, just north of the Kaibab Trailhead on the right (west) side of the road at the Widforss Trailhead. The dirt road is 17 miles one way and is impassible until July when the last of the snow melts and the mud dries out. Even when it's dry, you'll need experience at driving back roads in remote areas as well as a high clearance vehicle. Once there, you'll have a 300-degree view of the east-central Grand Canyon, including Sagittarius Ridge, Confucius and Mencius temples, the Crystal Creek area to the east, and the Shinumo Creek area and Powell Plateau to the west.

Toroweap

Toroweap is located on the North Rim in the central part of the Grand Canyon, far to the west of North Rim Village. At Toroweap Overlook, three-thousand foot sheer red rock cliffs drop almost directly to the Colorado River. This is a remote area and is difficult to reach, but for those visitors willing to travel long dirt roads, it's worth it.

There are no services of any type in the Toroweap area and all visitors must bring all food, water, and other supplies with them. The portion of the access road within the park is not recommended for low-clearance passenger vehicles.

From Kanab, Utah, drive 7 miles south on US 89A. Turn right on Arizona 389. Drive 8.3 miles west, and then turn right on dirt County Road 109 (Mount Trumbull Road). After 37 miles, stay left on CR 5. Drive 6 miles, and then stay left on CR 115. Continue 14 miles, passing the Toroweap Ranger Station, to Toroweap Overlook and Campground.

The primitive campground has 11 sites and is located along the access road just before the viewpoint. Water is not available and campers must bring their own firewood. Gathering firewood is prohibited.

At Toroweap, the dramatic landscape includes nearby Vulcans Throne, an old volcanic cinder cone, which is back-dropped by the equally volcanic Uinkaret Mountains. About 500,000 years ago, these volcanoes spewed red-hot lava into the Colorado River, filling the inner gorge with steam and ultimately creating a series of lava dams 1,200 feet high and sixty miles long. These dams, which created lakes that flooded much of the Grand Canyon, have been eroded away almost without a trace by the river.

Lava Falls Rapid, on the river about a mile downstream of Toroweap Overlook, is a visible and audible remnant of the catastrophic events of the geologic past. One of the hardest rapids on the river to run, the river drops thirty seven feet over and among ominous black rocks the size of small houses. The notorious rapids is not itself the remains of a lava dam, but instead formed where boulders washed down from Prospect Canyon and piled up in the Colorado River.

You can view a map of Toroweap here:
http://bit.ly/1TwRPbl

Photography Secrets

Why Didn't my Photo Come Out?

Many visitors to the Grand Canyon arrive after a drive up from I-40 and spend just a few hours at the rim, often during the middle of the day during the summer. The sun is high in the sky and floods the canyon with harsh light that washes out the colorful rock formations. It's far better to shoot early or late in the day, when the light is softer.

It's Not Your Equipment

Though the features on pro or semi-pro single lens reflex cameras are designed for versatility and flexibility in many different shooting situations, you can make stunning photographs with modest equipment as long as you understand its limitations. All but the cheapest point-and-shoot-cameras have computer-designed lenses that are remarkably sharp. And you don't need a lot of megapixels either. Large posters can be made from five megapixel images. Most smart phones have better cameras than that!

Seeing the Light

The human eye is a remarkable instrument. It is far more sensitive to light than any camera and also has an extremely sophisticated processor- the brain. The brain processes what we see into what we expect to see, based on what we've already experienced. This means we don't see the strong blue cast to the mid-day light on someone's face caused by the strong blue light from the open sky. We also don't see that scraggly tree branch sticking into our picture when we take it, only the towering rock temple dominating the frame.

Composition in Thirds

The placement of objects within your photo should create a pattern that is pleasing to the eye and draw the viewer into the image. Remember the rule of thirds, which states that major objects such as people, trees, rock formations, or the horizon should be placed one-third of the way in from the edge of the frame rather than in the center. Centered subjects make for dull photos. Action subjects such as hikers or cyclists should be positioned at the one-third point and should be moving into the remaining two-thirds of the frame. In other words, give them space.

Simplify

When composing your shot, eliminate distractions. Include as little in the frame as you can and still tell the story that you're trying to convey to your viewers. Move closer to your subject or use a telephoto lens or setting. Watch out for wide-angle lenses or settings. Used carefully, wide-angle lenses can create breathtaking images that sweep the viewer from intimate detail in the foreground to broad landscapes in the background, but they can also be loaded with irrelevant clutter.

Golden Light

Experienced landscape photographers know about the *golden hours*, the hour after sunrise and the hour before sunset when the sun is low to the horizon and the light is filtered by the atmosphere into soft, warm tones. At the Grand Canyon, rock formations leap into three dimensions and seem to glow with inner fire. Shadows and haze fill the depths and add an aura of mystery.

During the summer, you'll have to rise early or stay out late to catch the golden hours. During the spring and fall when the days are shorter, it's less work to get out during the golden hours. And even the mid-day light is softer due to the lower sun angle. Winter is one of the best times to photograph the

Grand Canyon. The sun is at its lowest and snow on the rims and terraces brings out the colors and relief of the canyon to a remarkable degree.

Sunrise and Sunset Calculator:
http://aa.usno.navy.mil/data/docs/RS_OneDay.php

Sun and Moon Azimuth Calculator:
http://aa.usno.navy.mil/data/docs/AltAz.php

The Photographer's Ephemeris: photoephemeris.com

Where to Shoot

If your time is limited, walk to Mather Point from the Grand Canyon Visitor Center. Then try walking east along the Rim Trail, and shoot back toward Mather Point itself. A shot of the long promontory with people crowding the guard rails is especially effective early in the morning. Another option is to walk the Rim Trail from El Tovar Hotel east toward Yavapai Point. You'll get a variety of views and lots of people for interest. As the view faces mainly northwest until you get to Yavapai Point, this section of the Rim Trail has the best light late from afternoon until sunset.

South Rim

For sunrise, try Pima, Mohave, Hopi, Mather, Yaki, Moran, and Lipan points. For sunset, consider Powell, Trailview, Yaki, Grandview, and Lipan points. Yaki Point is good for shots of hikers on the upper Kaibab Trail. And don't forget the many historic buildings in Grand Canyon Village, including El Tovar Hotel, Bright Angel Lodge, and the old railway station.

North Rim

Bright Angel Point, the most popular viewpoint on the North Rim, is one of the worst for photography. Fortunately, Point Imperial, Cape Royal, and Angels Window more than make up for it. Point Imperial offers a close view of Mount Hayden and the cliff-bound head of Nankoweap Creek and is a good place for sunrise. Cape Royal is also best at sunrise and early in the day. Nearby Angels Window viewpoint is especially effective at sunset when the setting sun lights up the foreground buttes and the Palisades of the Desert to the east.

Backcountry

I'll admit I'm prejudiced, but limiting your photography to the rim viewpoints that are accessible by paved road barely lets you scratch the surface of the Grand Canyon. If you have the time and a high clearance vehicle, visits to backcountry viewpoints such as the South Bass Trailhead, Point Sublime, Fire Point, and Toroweap will pay off in dramatic shots taken from unusual perspectives.

Get Physical

To really explore the canyon photographically you have to explore it physically, which means hiking the trails and running the river. On the river with a raft to carry your gear, you can carry a lot of equipment but you won't want to endanger an expensive single lens reflex in the whitewater. One of the new waterproof, submersible point-and-shoots will let you get some great shots.

Day Hikes

You can day hike the upper parts of some of the trails from the rims and get to some interesting vantage points. Good places to start are the South Kaibab Trail to O'Neill Butte, the Grandview Trail to Horseshoe Mesa, and the Hermit Trail to Santa Maria Spring or Dripping Spring. On the North Rim, try the Transcept Trail.

Gear for Backpacking

Of course, really getting into the Grand Canyon on foot requires backpacking for two or more days. Because of weight, you can't carry much photo gear. One of the waterproof point-and-shoots makes a great backpacking camera. Or, as I generally prefer, you can carry a lightweight single lens reflex camera body (these are often classed as semi-pro cameras) and a wide-range zoom lenses. Some of these cameras are now moisture and dust-sealed, a feature formerly available only on the heavy pro cameras.

Batteries and Storage Cards

Unless you'll have access to a charger and a computer or image storage device every day, make certain you have enough memory cards and fully charged batteries to last the trip. Memory cards are cheap, so there's no excuse for running out of space. Camera batteries are not cheap but current cameras are much easier on batteries than older models.

Tip

You can greatly extend battery life by turning off the LCD monitor and using the viewfinder, if your camera has one. Also, turn off instant review and use the play button to selectively review photos as needed. In camp, resist the urge to edit your photos on the camera, unless you know you have plenty of battery power.

Drones

Remotely-controlled aerial vehicles, whether used for photography or any other purpose, are prohibited in Grand Canyon National Park and at Grand Canyon West.

Commercial Photography

Commercial photography or videography involving props, models, professional crews and casts, or set dressings requires a permit. Personal or professional photography involving no more than a tripod and that doesn't disrupt other visitors does not require a permit or a fee in any national park.

Commercial Photography Permits:
http://www.nps.gov/grca/parkmgmt/filming.htm

Explore the Stars

The Grand Canyon is located in the least-populated part of the 48 United States and the high elevation skies are clear and dry much of the time. As a result, the area has some of the darkest skies in the United States, perfect for enjoying the glories of the universe (nearby Flagstaff is one of the world's prime telescope sites, with two major observatories.)

Where to Go

Although the sky is stunning even from Grand Canyon Village, for the best observing choose a location that is open and away from all artificial light. Some of the best spots are Grandview and Lipan points on Desert View Drive. Hopi and Pima points on Hermit Road are good during the winter when you have car access- during spring, summer, and fall, the Hermit Shuttle is the only way to reach these points and it doesn't run after dark.

If you're staying in Grand Canyon Village at one of the lodges or Mather Campground and don't want to drive, walk out to the Rim Trail.

On the North Rim, Point Imperial is the best star gazing site. If you don't want to drive and you're staying at Grand Canyon Lodge, just walk out to Bright Angel Point. If you're camping in the North Rim Campground, Bright Angel Point is a bit longer walk.

If you're staying outside the North Rim of the park, at DeMotte Campground or Kaibab Lodge, just walk out into DeMotte Park.

When you arrive on site, especially if you drove or used a flashlight to find your way, allow 20 minutes for your eyes to adjust to the dark. This is especially important when looking at dim objects or a meteor shower.

When to Go

Although you can look at the stars any time of the year, winter nights are very cold. Spring, summer, and fall are the best times of the year. During late summer, the evening sky is sometimes obscured by remnants of the day's thunderstorm activity. Watch the weather forecast and pick a night that is predicted to be clear. Even high clouds dim the stars. Seeing individual stars and other objects is best on nights with a new moon, because a bright moon washes out faint objects. On the other hand, a night with a full or nearly full moon is good for learning the major constellations, as the dimmer stars are hidden and the constellations stand out more.

Moon Phase Calculator: stardate.org/nightsky/moon/

What to Bring

- Warm clothing, gloves, and hat

- Thermos with a hot drink

- A blanket, ground cloth, or reclining camp chair

- Binoculars- even small backpacking binoculars will review many more stars and sky objects

- Star chart- available at the park bookstores

- Flashlight with a red lens to preserve your night vision

What to Look For

Use a star chart to orient yourself to the sky and see what is above the horizon at the present date and time. Traditional star charts are often available at the visitor centers and can be set for the time and date. Star chart apps such as Google Sky Map turn your phone or tablet into a smart star chart- just hold your device up against the sky and the screen shows the portion you're looking at, with constellation lines and names, as well as star and planet names. Just don't forget to remove any protective cases with magnets- the star chart uses your device's magnetic compass to orient itself and won't work around any nearby magnets.

Milky Way

The Milky Way is a faint band of light across the entire sky composed of millions of stars that are too faint to see with the naked eye. These stars make up the Milky Way Galaxy, of which our Sun is a member star. When you're looking at the Milky Way, you are literally looking at our home galaxy edge-on.

Constellations

From ancient times, humans have found patterns in the stars. Today, 88 constellations are recognized, covering the entire sky. All stars and other objects are found within one of these constellations, which in modern usage define a precise region of the sky. About half the constellations are major, made up of bright stars in a easily recognizable pattern. Learning the major constellations is the first step to knowing your way around the night sky. A few of the major constellations to look for during a summer night around 9 PM:

Ursa Major, the Great Bear: Look north to find the "Big Dipper," a group of stars that make up a dipper hanging from its handle with the bowl pointing right. The Big Dipper is an asterism- a named group of stars within the Great Bear constellation. The lower two stars of the dipper are the "Pointer Stars." A line drawn to the right through the pointer star passes through Polaris, the North Star. In turn, the North Star forms the end of the handle of the "Little Dipper", part of the constellation Little Bear. The Little Dipper is much smaller and fainter than the Big Dipper.

Cassiopeia: To the right and below the North Star is a bright group of stars forming a sideways "W" in the sky.

Lyra: Nearly overhead in the summer sky, Lyra is a small but bright constellation representing a lyre, an ancient musical instrument. A nearly perfect triangle shares one star with a parallelogram. The very bright star at one point of the triangle is Vega, one of the brightest stars in the sky.

Sagittarius, the Archer: In the southern sky, near the horizon, look for a group of bright stars forming an almost-perfect teapot, complete with handle, lid, and spout.

Scorpius, the Scorpion: Just to the right of Sagittarius, a large group of stars looks like a huge scorpion, with a bright pair of stars on the left making up the stinger, and a small group of fainter stars on the upper right representing the head. The bright red star in the middle of the constellation is Antares, a giant red star that is the heart of the scorpion.

Meteors

Meteors, or "shooting stars," are small pieces of rock that enter our atmosphere from space at tremendous speeds. The streak of light is the object burning up in the atmosphere. Most meteors are the size of a speck of sand, but occasionally a larger one will create a spectacular "fireball" in the sky, bright enough to light up the ground around the observer. Most meteors are natural objects, but occasionally you may spot pieces of a man-made satellite burning up in the atmosphere. You can tell the difference by the color- natural meteors are yellow, orange, or red, while artificial objects are usually bluish or greenish.

Meteor showers appear at certain times of the year and the show may include dozens or even hundreds of meteors per hour. The best meteor showers are the Perseids in August, the Orionids in October, the Leonids in November, and the Geminds in December.

Major meteor showers: www.amsmeteors.org/showers.html

Planets

Five planets are visible to the naked eye- Mercury, Venus, Mars, Jupiter, and Saturn. Even small binoculars will show you the phases of Venus, the red color of Mars, the moons of Jupiter, and the rings of Saturn. Because the planets orbit the Sun at various speeds, they appear to move across the sky, but always along the Ecliptic, the plane of the solar system.

Planet finder: www.lightandmatter.com/planetfinder/en/

Satellites

There are thousands of artificial satellites orbiting the earth, and many are easily seen by the naked eye. The best time to observe satellites is just after dusk, when the observer is in the dark but sunlight still strikes the satellites high overhead. Lie on your back and let your gaze wander over a broad patch of sky, looking for a "star" that moves. Some satellites, such as the Iridium series and the International Space Station, are very bright and are in low orbits that cause them to move quickly across the sky.

Heavens Above is a good Web site for satellite information: www.heavens-above.com/

For the Kids

Kids (and many adults, for that matter) quickly get bored with looking over the rim. Luckily, the National Park Service has a number of excellent programs for kids and families, including ranger-led talks and hikes, the WebRanger program, and the Junior Ranger program.

The Rim Trail is for Families

Starting from the South Kaibab Trailhead just east of Grand Canyon Village and continuing to Hermits Rest at the west end of Hermit Road, the Rim Trail winds along the South Rim past most of the South Rim's viewpoints.

The Village, Kaibab and Hermit shuttles, which are free, stop at most of the viewpoints along the Rim Trail, so you can walk any portion of the trail one-way, then ride the shuttle between viewpoints, or back to your starting place.

Be a WebRanger!

You can become a National Park WebRanger, even if you're not at the Grand Canyon by pointing your browser to www.nps.gov/webrangers/. You can play more than 50 games, learn about the national parks, and share park stories and pictures with other WebRangers around the world.

Junior Ranger Programs

For a current list of all ranger programs, see Park News at https://www.nps.gov/grca/learn/news/index.htm.

Junior Rangers have fun learning about the Grand Canyon and the national park and represent the park to their friends and families. There are five ways you can become a Junior Ranger of Grand Canyon National Park and all are free of charge.

Ravens, Coyotes, and Scorpions!

To become a Junior Ranger, you must complete the requirements for your age group in the Junior Ranger Activity Booklet. You can get a booklet at any of the visitor centers or museums on the South or North rims, including Grand Canyon Visitor Center, Yavapai Observation Station, Tusayan Museum, Desert View Information Center, and the North Rim Visitor Center.

Requirements for completion include writing down your observations and impressions, writing poems, answering questions about the park, and attending a free program led by a park ranger. This is a year-round program. There are different Junior Ranger Awards for these age groups:

- Ages 4 to 7: Raven Award

- Ages 8 to 10: Coyote Award

- Ages 11 and up: Scorpion Award

When you complete the requirements, bring the activity booklet to any visitor center or ranger station. A ranger will review your booklet, and issue an Official Grand Canyon Junior Ranger Certificate and Badge. Take your Junior Ranger Certificate to any park bookstore, and you can buy a sew-on patch to go with your Junior Ranger Award.

Phantom Rattler Junior Ranger

This is a special program for kids age 4 to 14. Only kids who ride mules or hike to Phantom Ranch at the bottom of the Grand Canyon can become Phantom Rattler Junior Rangers. After getting to Phantom Ranch, complete the activities in the Junior Ranger Booklet.

Booklets are available at the Phantom Ranch Ranger Station, the canteen, or the campground. After completing the activities in the booklet, you'll receive your Junior Ranger Badge, Patch, and Certificate from a ranger at Phantom Ranch. This program is available all year.

Junior Ranger Dynamic Earth Adventure Hike

Available from mid-June through mid-August, kids 8 to 14 can join a park ranger on a hike down the Hermit Trail. Up to two miles round-trip, this is a strenuous hike, so bring water and sunscreen and wear good hiking shoes.

The Adventure Hike begins at 9:00 AM at the Hermits Rest Bell, next to the Hermits Rest Shuttle Stop at the west end of Hermit Road. Board the Hermit Shuttle at the west end of Grand Canyon Village by 8:00 AM so you'll be on time.

After completing the 2-1/2-hour program, you'll be eligible to buy a Junior Ranger Adventure Hike patch. This program also satisfies the ranger activity requirement for the Junior Ranger Activity Booklet.

Junior Ranger Discovery Pack

This program is for kids 8 to 14 and their families. Young naturalists attend a 1-1/2-hour ranger-led program, which meets at Park Headquarters at 9:00 AM mid-June through Labor Day weekend. A park ranger will help kids and their families learn to use the tools in the Discovery Pack, which include binoculars, a hand lens, a journal, and field guides.

After the talk, families take the Discovery Pack with them while they explore the park for the day, completing the journal as they discover plants, animals, and birds. At the end of the day, return the Discovery Pack to a ranger, who will review the Discovery Pack Field Journal. This program also satisfies the ranger activity requirement for the Junior Ranger Activity Booklet.

North Rim Junior Ranger Discovery Pack

A Junior Ranger Discovery Pack program is also offered on the North Rim during the summer months. For information, check the Park News page at
https://www.nps.gov/grca/learn/news/index.htm.

Junior Ranger Family Programs

These programs fulfill the requirement to participate in one ranger-led activity for the Raven, Coyote, or Scorpion Junior Ranger badges. They are offered from June through August.

Storytime Adventure

For kids from 2 to 6 years, this program is held on the lawn behind El Tovar Hotel from 1:30 to 2:00 PM daily, June 8 through September 1. A park ranger will read from his or her favorite Grand Canyon children's books, and require active audience participation.

Way Cool Stuff for Kids and Kids Rock!

Both programs are geared for kids from ages 6 to 12. Way Cool Stuff for Kids starts at 4:00 PM at the Shrine of the Ages parking lot A, and runs June through September 1.

Kids Rock! starts at the same place at 10:00 AM and runs June through August 16. Each program lasts one hour. Come prepared to have fun and learn something new! Previous topics have included:

- Bizarre Bats

- Amazing Mountain Lions

- Fire in a Forest

- Water in Our World

- Archeology

- Tremendous Trees

- Animal Tracking

- Astronomy

- Arts and Crafts

Lodging and Restaurants

Grand Canyon Village on the South Rim and the gateway communty of Tusayan 10 miles south of the rim have most of the lodging and restaurants that are in or near the park. The North Rim has one lodge, Grand Canyon Lodge, within the park, and two outside the park on AZ 67- Jacob Lake Inn and Kaibab Lodge. All of the North Rim lodges have restaurants. There is also a resort at the bottom of the canyon along the Kaibab Trail, Phantom Ranch, which can be accessed by hiking the trail or by mule trip.

Advance Reservations Recommended

Rooms are scarce during the busy period from March through November, so be sure to make advance reservations. It's possible you can walk in and pick up a last-minute cancellation, but don't count on it during high season.

Tip

During the winter, lodging is much easier to come by, and rates often drop as well, just more good reasons to visit in winter if you can.

Staying in Nearby Cities

Since lodging can be difficult to come by inside the park and in the gateway communities of Tusayan and Jacob Lake from March through November, consider staying in the larger towns further from the park. Williams is about an hour's drive from the South Rim. Flagstaff, is about an hour and a quarter from the South Rim. Kanab, Utah, and Fredonia, Arizona, are about an hour and forty-five minutes from the North Rim.

Lodging Within the Park

South Rim and Phantom Ranch

Xanterra operates the South Rim lodges and Phantom Ranch-for reservations, call 888-297-2727 or 303-297-2757, or go to the Xanterra website at www.grandcanyonlodges.com.. For same day reservations, call 928-638-2631.

El Tovar Hotel: One of the classic national park lodges and a National Historic Landmark, El Tovar opened in 1905 and was renovated in 2014. The hotel features a dining room that is open for breakfast, lunch, and dinner. It is located on the South Rim in Grand Canyon Village.

Bright Angel Lodge was designed by famed Southwestern architect Mary Jane Colter in 1935 as a rustic lodge and is also a National Historic Landmark. It is located on the South Rim at the west end of Grand Canyon Village. There are two restaurants.

Kachina Lodge is a modern lodge located on the South Rim between Bright Angel Lodge and El Tovar. Some rooms have partial Canyon views. It is a short walk to the restaurants at El Tovar and Bright Angel Lodge.

Thunderbird Lodge is another modern lodge on the rim between El Tovar and Bright Angel Lodge. As with Kachina Lodge, some rooms have partial Canyon views. It is a short walk to the restaurants at El Tovar and Bright Angel Lodge.

Maswik Lodge is located at the southwest corner of Grand Canyon Village, about 1/4 mile from the South Rim. It is a motel-style lodge with a cafeteria and sports bar. Rustic cabins are available during the summer.

Yavapai Lodge is the largest lodge on the South Rim within the park, and is located near Market Plaza in Grand Canyon Village, about 1/2 mile from the South Rim. There is a cafe which is open all day, and the park

Visitor Center is close by at Grand Canyon Visitor Center. Market Plaza has a grocery store, bank, and post office.

Phantom Ranch is a unique lodge designed by Mary Jane Colter and is located along Bright Angel Creek and the North Kaibab Trail, just north of the Colorado River. It is the only lodge located at the bottom of the canyon. Phantom Ranch can only be reached by foot, mule, or via a Colorado River trip. Overnight mule trips include a stay at Phantom Ranch- all others must make reservations for lodging and meals in advance. The canteen serves snacks and beverages.

North Rim

Grand Canyon Lodge is the only lodge on the North Rim within the park, and it is operated by Forever Resorts. It is located near Bright Angel Point on the North Rim. A National Historic Landmark, Grand Canyon Lodge is unique among national park lodges in that the main building doesn't have guest rooms. Instead, as you enter, you get your first glimpse of the Grand Canyon through the sweeping view windows of the veranda. Separate cabins provide the accommodations, and there is a dining room off the veranda. To make reservations, call 877-386-4383 or 480-337-1320.

Forever Resorts website:
http://foreverlodging.com/lodging.cfm?PropertyKey=181

Lodging Outside the Park

South Rim

There are a large number of motels and hotels located in Tusayan, about 10 miles south of the South Rim just outside the park, several in Valle, about 30 miles south of the South Rim, and in the cities of Williams and Flagstaff along I-40.

For central lodging reservations, call 800-916-8530, or visit the Grand Canyon Hotels and Lodges website: www.grandcanyon.com/hotels.html

North Rim

There are two lodges on the Kaibab Plateau north of the North Rim along AZ 67, the access highway.

Jacob Lake Inn is located at the junction of US 89A and AZ 67 about 43 miles north of the North Rim. The inn was built in 1923 and is nestled in the towering pines of the Kaibab National Forest. Jacob Lake Inn has a cafe featuring locally baked goods, as well as a gift shop with local native arts and crafts, and a gas station. The Kaibab National Forest Visitor Center is just south of the inn. For reservations, call 928-643-7232, or visit the Jacob Lake Inn website: www.jacoblake.com

Kaibab Lodge is located on the edge of DeMotte Park in the Kaibab National Forest, about 10 miles north of the North Rim along AZ 67. The lodge has a restaurant, and there is a gas station and general store across the highway. Kaibab Lodge is open from mid-May through mid-October, and closed in the winter. For reservations, call 928-638-2389, or visit the Kaibab Lodge website: www.kaibablodge.com

Restaurants and Dining

All of the lodges listed above have dining at the lodge or nearby. In addition, the towns of Tusayan, Valle, Williams, and Flagstaff, south of the South Rim, also have numerous cafes, restaurants, and fast food. In the area of the North Rim, the nearest towns with restaurants and fast food are Fredonia on US 89A and Page on US 89, and Kanab, Utah, on US 89. See the Grand Canyon Area Map.

Camping

Both Grand Canyon National Park and the surrounding Kaibab National Forest have developed vehicle campgrounds. There are no vehicle campgrounds within Grand Canyon-Parashant National Monument or the Havasupai or Hualapai reservations. All of the campgrounds except for Toroweap charge a nightly fee.

> **Tip**
>
> I strongly recommend getting advance reservations for those campgrounds that accept them. Campgrounds at and near the Grand Canyon fill up quickly during peak camping season, May through October. If you are in an RV, consider camping at Mather Campground on the South Rim during the winter. (It's a bit cold for tent camping unless you are really into winter camping- lows are usually 10-20F and can be subzero.)

Another option is camping in the national forest campgrounds near Williams or Flagstaff. There are numerous campgrounds on both forests (see my FalconGuide, *Camping Arizona*). These campgrounds usually fill up on summer weekends, but during the week, and during spring and fall, it's easier to get a site.

Backcountry Camping

Except for those holding a backcountry camping permit, camping is limited to developed campgrounds within the national park. However, you can camp just about anywhere on Kaibab National Forest adjacent to the park on both rims, except near highways and a few other areas that are closed. If you're comfortable driving a few miles on gravel roads, you can have an undeveloped camp spot all to yourself. I suggest that you stop at the US Forest Service office at the north end of Tusayan, or the Visitor Center at Jacob Lake, and pick up a Kaibab National Forest map.

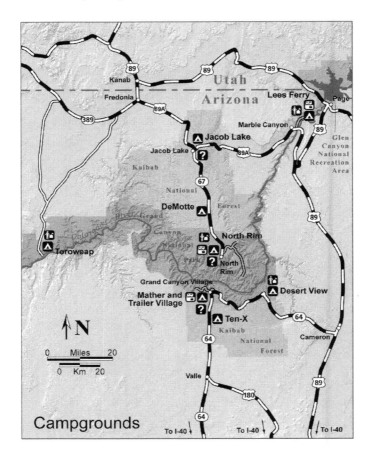

South Rim

Mather Campground

Location: Grand Canyon Village near Market Plaza

Season: All year

Units: 315

Tents: Yes

RVs and Trailers: Up to 30 feet

Dump Station: Yes, except in winter

Hookups: No

Water: Yes

Showers: Yes, at Market Plaza

Self-Serve Laundry: Yes, at Market Plaza

Handicap-Accessible: Yes

Management: Grand Canyon National Park,
www.nps.gov/grca

Reservations: National Recreation Reservation Service,
www.recreation.gov, 877-444-6777

Mather Campground is the largest in the Grand Canyon area and the only one open all year. Pets are allowed but must be leashed at all times and must not be left unattended. Wood gathering is not permitted, but wood is available at the general store in Market Plaza. Reservations are strongly recommended during the busy season from March through October.

Trailer Village

Location: Grand Canyon Village near Market Plaza

Season: All year

Units: 78

Grand Canyon Tips

Tents: No

RVs and Trailers: Yes

Dump Station: Yes, except in winter

Hookups: Yes, all sites

Water: Yes

Showers: Yes, at Market Plaza

Self-Serve Laundry: Yes, at Market Plaza

Handicap-Accessible: Yes

Management: Grand Canyon National Park,
www.nps.gov/grca

Reservations: 888-297-2727 or 303-297-2757

Trailer Village is located next to Mather Campground in Grand Canyon Village.

Desert View Campground

Location: Desert View

Season: May to mid-October

Units: 50

Tents: Yes

RVs and Trailers: Yes, up to 30 feet

Dump Station: No

Hookups: No

Water: Yes

Showers: No

Self-Serve Laundry: No

Handicap-Accessible: Yes

Management: Grand Canyon National Park,
www.nps.gov/grca

Reservations: First-come, first-served

Located at Desert View at the east end of Desert View Drive, this campground can handle some RVs up to 30 feet but most sites are designed for smaller RVs, trailers, or tents. Pets are allowed but must be leashed at all times and cannot be left unattended.

Ten-X Campground

Location: Two miles south of Tusayan

Season: May to September

Units: 70

Tents: Yes

RVs and Trailers: Yes, up to 40 feet

Dump Station: No

Hookups: No

Water: Yes

Showers: No

Self-Serve Laundry: No

Handicap-Accessible: Yes

Management: Kaibab National Forest,
www.fs.usda.gov/kaibab

Reservations: National Recreation Reservation Service,
recreation.gov, 877-444-6777

This campground is two miles south of Tusayan on the east side of AZ 64. Firewood may be collected outside the campground. Two group campsites are available and must be reserved in advance.

Lees Ferry

Lees Ferry Campground

Location: Five miles from Marble Canyon at Lees Ferry

Season: All year

Units: 54

Tents: Yes

RVs and Trailers: Yes

Dump Station: Yes

Hookups: No

Water: Yes

Showers: No

Self-Serve Laundry: At Marble Canyon

Handicap-Accessible: Yes

Management: Glen Canyon National Recreation Area, www.nps.gov/glca, 928-608-6200

Reservations: First-come, first-served

This campground is located at the head of Marble Canyon at historic Lees Ferry, where most Grand Canyon river trips begin. Fishing is popular on the Colorado River, and a boat ramp is available. A general store and gas station are located five miles away at Marble Canyon.

North Rim

North Rim Campground

Location: North Rim Village

Season: Mid-May to mid-October

Units: 83

Tents: Yes

RVs and Trailers: Yes

Dump Station: Yes

Hookups: No

Water: Yes

Showers: At campground entrance

Self-Serve Laundry: At campground entrance

Handicap-Accessible: Yes

Management: Grand Canyon National Park,
www.nps.gov/grca

Reservations: National Recreation Reservation Service,
www.recreation.gov, 877-444-6777

North Rim Campground is located just north of the North Rim Village on the entrance road. Collection of firewood is not allowed, but wood may be purchased at the adjacent general store. Because sites fill up early, reservations are strongly recommended.

Toroweap Campground

Location: Toroweap Overlook

Season: All year, but access road may be impassable after
a winter storm

Units: 9

Tents: Yes

RVs and Trailers: No

Dump Station: No

Hookups: No

Water: No

Showers: No

Self-Serve Laundry: No

Handicap-Accessible: No

Management: Grand Canyon National Park,
www.nps.gov/grca

Reservations: First-come, first-served

This campground is located just north of Toroweap Overlook. There are 9 sites, available on a first-come, first-served basis. Water is not available. See the Toroweap chapter for more information on the area.

DeMotte Campground

Location: On AZ 67, 25 miles south of Jacob Lake

Season: Mid-May through October, depending on snowfall

Units: 38

Tents: Yes

RVs and Trailers: Yes

Dump Station: No

Hookups: No

Water: Yes

Showers: No

Self-Serve Laundry: No

Handicap-Accessible: Yes

Management: Kaibab National Forest,
www.fs.usda.gov/kaibab

Reservations: First-come, first-served

DeMotte Campground is seven miles north of the North Entrance to Grand Canyon National Park, and is located on the edge of beautiful DeMotte Park. Nearby Kaibab Lodge has rooms and a restaurant, and there is a general store and service station across the highway.

Jacob Lake Campground

Location: Jacob Lake at the junction of US 89A and AZ 67

Season: Mid-May through October, depending on snowfall

Units: 51

Tents: Yes

RVs and Trailers: Yes

Dump Station: No

Hookups: No

Water: Yes

Showers: No

Self-Serve Laundry: No

Handicap-Accessible: Yes

Management: Kaibab National Forest, www.fs.usda.gov/kaibab

Reservations: First-come, first-served

This campground is located in the ponderosa pine forest across from Jacob Lake Lodge. The lodge has rooms, a restaurant, a general store, and a service station.

Hiking and Backpacking

As a life-long hiker and backpacker, I'll admit right up front that I'm totally biased, but walking and hiking is one of the very best ways to see the Grand Canyon. And just by being a hiker, you leave the crowds behind. Over five million people visit the park each year, but only a few hundred thousand people explore Grand Canyon's stunning wilderness backcountry. And most of those hikers are found on the Kaibab and Bright Angel trails, the only maintained trails below the rim in the park.

You don't have to be super fit to take a walk or a hike, but you do have to be prepared. Every year, people get into serious trouble hiking in the Canyon. The most common problem is dehydration, as mentioned earlier. Arizona's summer air is extremely dry, and your body loses moisture rapidly, often without any visible sweating. If not reversed, or better yet prevented, by drinking plenty of water and eating light snacks, dehydration leads to heat exhaustion and sun stroke. The symptoms of heat exhaustion are difficult to recognize in yourself, and unless experienced, other members of your party may not notice until it's too late and you are incapacitated and unable to hike. If untreated, heat exhaustion leads to sun stroke, which is often fatal unless the victim is immediately transported to a hospital.

So don't take water lightly. Take plenty. Your body needs as much as two gallons a day doing strenuous exercise in the Arizona summer heat. Also eat salty, high energy snacks such as nuts and fruit to keep your electrolytes up.

For any backcountry hike, which means anything below the rim or away from the established rim trails, bring the Ten Essentials:

- Plenty of water

- Extra food

- Sunglasses

- Sunscreen

- Map

- Compass

- Knife

- Lighter or fire starter

- Rain gear and extra clothes

- First aid kit

Tip

Take it easy, no matter how experienced you are at hiking in the mountains. The desert is different. It's not only drier and hotter, but most of the Grand Canyon's trails are unmaintained and are much rougher and slower than trails in other national parks. Travel at the speed of the slowest member of your group, and stop often to enjoy the view and take pictures.

Hiking Permits

Permits are not required for day hikes in Grand Canyon National Park (except for group trail running), or for day hikes, backpacking, or camping on the lands surrounding the park, including the Kaibab National Forest and Grand Canyon-Parashant National Monument.

Tip

I strongly recommend that you get an advance reservation for your backpacking trip, especially during spring break, Easter weekend, and Thanksgiving. The most popular backpacking trails are the North and South Kaibab, Bright Angel, Hermit, and Grandview.

A backcountry permit is required for all overnight or longer hikes anywhere in the park. Permits for popular areas can be difficult to obtain, so it is advisable to apply well in advance, and have alternate trip plans.

The permit system is complex- check the park website for details:www.nps.gov/grca/planyourvisit/backcountry-permit.htm.

Permits are required for all access to the Hualapai Indian Reservation and the Havasupai Indian Reservation, including hiking, backpacking, and camping.

Here's a short list of some of the day hikes and backpack trips I recommend. For more information on these hikes, see my book *Grand Canyon Guide*.

Guided Hikes

If you don't feel up to organizing your own hike, join a ranger-led day hike. For hikes with an educational emphasis, consider joining a trip led by the Grand Canyon Field Institute. And finally, you can go with a commercial guide service authorized by the National Park Service. For more information, see the park's Guided Hikes page.

Maps

For overview maps of the trails, see GrandCanyonGuide.net or my book, *Grand Canyon Guide*. There are links to the online maps at the end of each hike description.

Day Hikes

South Rim

South Kaibab Trail

A great day hike starts at the South Kaibab Trailhead (accessible only via the Kaibab Shuttle) to Cedar Ridge, a distance of 1.5 miles one way. There are panoramic views of O'Neill Butte and the Canyon as the trail comes out onto a ridge. Remember, the return hike is all uphill and much harder. There is no water along the trail. Do not attempt to hike to the river and back in one day!

You can view an online trail map here: http://www.grandcanyonguide.net/?q=content/upper-south-kaibab-trail

Hermit Trail

This unmaintained trail starts from Hermits Rest at the end of the Hermit Road. Good destinations are Santa Maria Spring, which is 2.5 miles each way, and Dripping Spring, which is 3.5 miles each way. Neither spring is reliable, so carry your own water. Both destinations offer excellent views of Hermit Canyon. Do not attempt to hike to the river and back in one day!

You can view an online trail map here: http://www.grandcanyonguide.net/?q=content/hermit-trail

Grandview Trail

This trail starts from Grandview Point on Desert View Drive. Horseshoe Mesa, 3.0 miles each way, is a great destination. The Grandview Trail is unmaintained and is much rougher and slower going than the Kaibab or Bright Angel trails. You can easily spend a few hours exploring the historic mining district. Caution: Stay out of old mine shafts.

You can view an online trail map here: http://www.grandcanyonguide.net/?q=content/grandview-trail

Arizona Trail, South Rim

A section of the 800-mile Arizona Trail follows the Coconino Rim southeast from Grandview Fire Lookout on the Tusayan District of the Kaibab National Forest. To reach this trailhead, drive east on Desert View Drive to the Grandview Point junction. Continue 2.0 miles east on Desert Drive, and then turn right onto the Coconino Rim Road. Drive this dirt road 1.2 miles. You'll see the Arizona Trail trailhead on the left, just after crossing the park boundary into the national forest.

Follow the Arizona Trail east from the trailhead. The trail wanders through the pleasant mixed forest of ponderosa pine, pinyon pine, and juniper as it loosely follows the Coconino

Rim. A good destination for a day hike is a point 3.1 miles, one-way, from the trailhead, where the Arizona Trail reaches a sharply-defined, eastward-facing section of the Coconino Rim with excellent views.

For more information on the Arizona Trail, see the Arizona Trail Association website: www.aztrail.org

You can view an online trail map here: http://www.grandcanyonguide.net/?q=content/arizona-trail-coconino-rim

North Rim

Ken Patrick Trail

This trail connects Point Imperial with the North Kaibab Trailhead, a distance of 10 miles. If you plan to hike the entire trail, it is best to hike it one way with a car shuttle. The trail skirts the rim after leaving Point Imperial, then crosses the Point Imperial Road and wanders through the forest to the North Kaibab Trailhead.

You can view an online trail map here: http://www.grandcanyonguide.net/?q=content/ken-patrick-trail

North Kaibab Trail

The park's trans-canyon trail, the North Kaibab Trail starts from the North Kaibab Trailhead just north of the village, descends into Roaring Springs Canyon, and then follows Bright Angel Creek to Phantom Ranch and the Colorado River, a distance of 14 miles one-way and a descent of 5,950 feet. Do not attempt to hike to the river and back in one day! A day hike to Supai Tunnel and back is a good short day hike. This hike is 2.0 miles each way and a descent of 1,400 feet. For an all day hike, you can hike down to Roaring Springs and back, which is 4.7 miles each way and a descent of 3,050 feet.

You can view an online trail map here: http://www.grandcanyonguide.net/?q=content/ken-patrick-trail

Arizona Trail- North Canyon Loop

This strenuous 3.7-mile loop hike uses sections of both the North Canyon and Arizona trails to loop down into the head of North Canyon, past a spring, and then back along the rim of North Canyon. To reach the trailhead, start from Jacob Lake at the junction of US 89A and AZ 67, and drive 26 miles south on Arizona 67 to DeMotte Park. Turn left on Forest Road 611 and follow the signs four miles to East Rim View.

Descend into North Canyon via the North Canyon Trail, which descends 1,400 feet in about 1.4 miles to the bottom of the canyon. Then turn right, and follow the trail up the bed of the canyon. As the trail nears the head of North Canyon, it veers right and climbs steeply up the west fork, passing North Canyon Spring, and continues to the rim, a distance of 1.6 miles. Turn right and follow the Arizona Trail north 1.7 miles to East Rim View.

For an alternative, easier hike, follow the Arizona Trail south along the rim of North Canyon for 1.7 miles, one way, and then return the way you came.

For more information on the Arizona Trail, see the Arizona Trail Association website: www.aztrail.org.

You can view an online trail map here:
http://www.grandcanyonguide.net/?q=content/arizona-trail-north-canyon-loop

Backpack Trips

Backpacking in the Grand Canyon is extremely rewarding for those who are both experienced and equipped. Gain experience by doing the day hikes in the previous section before trying your first multi-day trip.

Trails and routes in the canyon are defined by the persistent horizontal cliff bands, and even though you may be able to see a spring or stream from above, you may not be able to reach it. For its size, Grand Canyon has very few trails. Only the Kaibab and Bright Angel Trails are maintained- the remaining dozen are leftover prospector trails, maintained primarily by use. These trails are generally unsigned and may fade out without warning, or be confused by multiple routes.

The best seasons for backpacking in the Grand Canyon are spring and fall, when the canyon temperatures are moderate. Winter can be a good season as well, though the top several thousand feet of the trails may be snow-covered.

Avoid hiking during the summer heat, from May through September! Temperatures reach 110 degrees F in the lower parts of the canyon and any mistakes you make, especially with regard to water, quickly become fatal.

Refer to my website, GrandCanyonGuide.net for a list of hiking guide books and maps.

Tip

If you have never done a backpack trip in the Grand Canyon, I strongly suggest you start with the Kaibab-Bright Angel Loop. Many backpack trips in the Grand Canyon require difficult cross-country hiking. Unless a member of your party is an experienced Grand Canyon backpacker, spend some time hiking the backcountry trails and learning how to route find in the canyon before attempting any cross-country hike.

South Rim

Kaibab-Bright Angel Loop

The classic first-time backpack trip in the Canyon, this loop is often done as an overnighter, but there's so much to explore that you could easily use up five days. The loop starts from the Kaibab Trailhead and returns to the Bright Angel Trailhead. Since both of these South Rim trailheads are served by free year-round shuttle buses, leave your car at the Backcountry Office.

The South Kaibab Trail is the best way to start the loop, because the trail follows ridges much of the way and offers great views during the steady descent. Allow half a day for the hike to Phantom Ranch and Bright Angel Campground.

You can use Bright Angel Campground (or Phantom Ranch, if you make reservations) as a base for exploration up the North Kaibab Trail to Ribbon Falls and Phantom Canyon's impressive gorge. Because of flash flood danger, stay out of Phantom Canyon during stormy weather. Make time for a side hike up the Clear Creek Trail to the Tonto Plateau for stunning views of Granite Gorge.

Return to the South Rim via the Silver Bridge, River Trail, and Bright Angel Trail. Though longer than the South Kaibab Trail, this route has gentler grades and a variety of scenery. You could also camp at Indian Garden, and spend some time doing a side hike out to Plateau Point. Other options for exploration include the Tonto Trail to the east and to the west.

You can view an online trail map here:
http://www.grandcanyonguide.net/?q=content/kaibab-bright-angel-loop

Boucher-Hermit Loop

This great loop hike starts from Hermits Rest at the end of the Hermit Road and is a good introduction to backcountry hiking on unmaintained trails. Use the free Hermit Shuttle to reach the trailhead, except during winter when the shuttle is not running. (There is trailhead parking down a short gravel road beyond the main parking lot.) This loop makes a nice three day trip, though you could easily expand it to four or five days.

Follow the Hermit Trail down through the Coconino Sandstone past the junction with the Waldron Trail. At the second junction, turn left onto the Dripping Spring Trail, and follow this trail across the top of the Supai Group cliffs at the head of Hermit Canyon to the Boucher Trail. Turn right, and follow the Boucher Trail along the top of the Supai, down into the head of White Creek, through the saddle next to White Butte, and eventually down to the Tonto Trail. Take the Tonto Trail a short distance west into Boucher Creek. The ruins of the Hermit's (Louis Boucher) mine and cabin are still present near the creek, which has permanent water- if not at the trail crossing, then a short distance downstream. The cross-country hike down Boucher Creek to the river is easy, and only takes a few hours round-trip.

The hike continues east on the Tonto Trail, which winds around Travertine Canyon before reaching Hermit Creek and its permanent water. Here, you can hike cross-country down Hermit Creek to the Colorado River to catch a view of the huge waves of Hermit Rapid, and also spend some time exploring the remains of Hermit Camp. This tourist camp was the main resort below the rim until the opening of Phantom Ranch on the Kaibab Trail. It was supplied by a 4,000-foot aerial tramway from Pima Point on the South Rim.

Hike east on the Tonto Trail to reach the junction with the Hermit Trail, your trail out of the Canyon. After a long climb up the Tonto slopes, a tight series of switchbacks ascend the Redwall Limestone at Cathedral Stairs. The Hermit Trail then climbs across the Supai Group slopes, switchbacking up through breaks in the cliff bands, and eventually reaches the old rest house and watering trough at Santa Maria Spring (the spring is seasonal and not reliable.) After climbing through the Esplanade Sandstone at the top of the Supai Group, the Hermit Trail passes the junctions with the Dripping Spring and Waldron trails, and continues to the rim at Hermits Rest.

You can view an online trail map here:
http://www.grandcanyonguide.net/?q=content/boucher-hermit-loop

North Rim

North Kaibab Trail

While many backpackers focus on using the trans-canyon Kaibab Trail to hike rim to rim, there's a lot to do along the North Kaibab Trail itself. Using the two campgrounds, Cottonwood Camp and Bright Angel Campground, as bases, you can explore such enticing places as upper Bright Angel Canyon (the route of the original North Kaibab Trail), The Transept, Ribbon Falls, Phantom Canyon, and the Clear Creek Trail. A nice overnight hike from the North Kaibab Trailhead is to Cottonwood Camp and back, but you could easily spend a week in the area.

You can view an online trail map here:
http://www.grandcanyonguide.net/?q=content/north-kaibab-trail-0

Nankoweap Trail

This long, rough trail is a challenge to most hikers, but it leads into the beautiful Nankoweap Creek area with its permanent stream and easy access to the river. There are two trailheads for the Nankoweap Trail; most hikers use the Saddle Mountain Trailhead. To reach this trailhead, turn south on Buffalo Ranch Road about a mile east of the point where US 89A climbs onto the Kaibab Plateau. This graded road is passable to most vehicles, except after a major storm. It's 27.4 miles south to the signed trailhead for the Saddle Mountain and Nankoweap trails.

Follow the Saddle Mountain Trail down into Saddle Canyon, where you'll come to a junction and stay right on the Nankoweap Trail. This trail continues up Saddle Canyon and eventually climbs up a ridge through ponderosa pine forest to reach a large saddle just west of Saddle Mountain. (The original, seldom-used upper Nankoweap Trail descends from the North Rim north of Point Imperial, and comes in from the right just above this saddle). The Nankoweap Trail descends into the Grand Canyon via a series of short switchbacks but soon levels out and follows a terrace at the base of the Esplanade Sandstone (the uppermost cliff in the Supai Group.) It stays at this level, descending slowly with the tilt in the rock strata, all the way to Tilted Mesa. There is one tricky place where the original trail construction has fallen away and the hiker-maintained trail crosses a short but steep slope above a cliff. This spot is usually no trouble when the trail is dry, but can be a problem when the trail is muddy.

Just above Tilted Mesa, the Nankoweap Trail descends a ridge through the remainder of the Supai Group, then turns right and switchbacks down a broad slope through the Redwall Limestone. The trail then heads generally southeast and comes out on the Tonto slope south of Tilted Mesa. It makes the final descent to Nankoweap Creek at the 3400-foot elevation contour. There are several spacious campsites here that you can use as a base for exploring Nankoweap Creek as well as south along the Horsethief Route. You can also follow Nankoweap Creek downstream to the Colorado River.

You can view an online trail map here:
http://www.grandcanyonguide.net/?q=content/nankoweap-trail

Thunder River

By far the most popular of the North Rim's non-maintained trails, the Thunder River Trail takes you into an area with interesting geology, the world's shortest river, and aptly-named Thunder Spring, which roars out of a cave in the Redwall Limestone. You can do this as an overnight hike, but most backpackers like to take longer because of the long drive to the trailhead. There are plenty of side hikes that you can do from the Thunder River area.

Fall is the best season for a hike to Thunder River. Summer is too hot, and the access road is often impassable during the winter and spring.

Most hikers use the shorter Bill Hall Trail from Monument Point rather than the original trailhead from Indian Hollow. To reach the Bill Hall Trailhead from Jacob Lake on US 89A, drive south on AZ 67 0.4 miles, and then turn right onto Forest Road 461. Drive 5.2 miles, and then turn right onto FR 462. Continue 3.3 miles, and then turn left onto FR 422. Drive 11.4 miles, and then turn right onto FR 425. Drive 10.3 miles, and then bear right onto FR 292, which is the main road. Continue 2.9 miles as the road becomes FR 292A and ends at the Bill Hall Trailhead.

The Bill Hall Trail (named after a ranger who died in an accident) heads west along the rim to Monument Point, then descends steeply off the rim south of the point. It then heads north along the Toroweap Formation terraces to a break in the Coconino Sandstone, where it descends abruptly to the west to meet the Thunder River Trail on the broad terrace of the Esplanade. Turn left at this junction and follow the Thunder River Trail as the trail works it way south around drainages west of Bridgers Knoll. The trail then turns west and descends to a saddle. Turning south, the Thunder River Trail descends the Redwall Limestone in a series of short, steep switchbacks, finally coming out onto gentler terrain in Surprise Valley. Stay left at two junctions with the trails to Deer Creek.

Surprise Valley is the top of a huge slump block, where a massive section of Redwall Limestone slid down and tilted as it dropped. Across the valley, the summit of Cogswell Butte consists of layers of Supai Group rocks on top of the Redwall slump block.

Continue east on the Thunder River Trail, which climbs a bit to reach the east rim of Surprise Valley. Here you are suddenly greeted with the roar of Thunder Spring bursting out of its Redwall Limestone cave to form Thunder River. The trail continues a steep descent alongside Thunder River past small campsites, and ends where Thunder River meets Tapeats Creek.

It's possible to explore cross-country upstream along Tapeats Creek, where you'll have to wade through a short narrows in the Tapeats Sandstone. A well-worn river-runner's trail leads down Tapeats Creek to the Colorado River. Another possible side hike starts at the junction with the Deer Creek Trail in Surprise Valley, and follows the Deer Creek Trail to Deer Valley.

You can view an online trail map here:
http://www.grandcanyonguide.net/?q=content/thunder-river

Fly the Canyon

Airplane and helicopter air tours over Grand Canyon are available from airports outside the national park. The following operators are all FAA-certified air carriers and offer air tours from Grand Canyon National Park Airport and other airports in the region.

Tip

When scheduling an overflight, try to be as flexible as you can with your dates. The Grand Canyon is located on a high plateau that makes its own weather, and conditions can change rapidly. All Grand Canyon air tour operators must fly specific routes and altitudes and even isolated low clouds and showers can cause air tours to cancel.

Grand Canyon National Park Airport

Grand Canyon Airlines: www.grandcanyonairlines.com, 866-235-9422

Grand Canyon Helicopters: www.grandcanyonhelicoptersaz.com, 702-835-8477

Maverick Helicopters: www.maverickhelicopter.com, 888-261-4414

Papillon Helicopters: www.papillon.com, 888-635-7272 or 702-736-7243

Westwind Air Service: www.westwindairservice.com, 888-869-0866

Page

Scenic Airlines: www.scenic.com, 866-235-9422 or 702-638-3300

Westwind Air Service: www.westwindairservice.com, 888-869-0866

Las Vegas and Grand Canyon West

Grand Canyon Helicopters: www.grandcanyonhelicoptersaz.com, 702-835-8477

Maverick Helicopters: www.maverickhelicopter.com, 888-261-4414 or 702-261-0007

Scenic Airlines: www.scenic.com, 866-235-9422 or 702-638-3300

Sundance Helicopters: www.sundancehelicopters.com, 800-653-1881

Phoenix

Westwind Air Service: www.westwindairservice.com, 888-869-0866

Sedona

Westwind Air Service: www.westwindairservice.com, 888-869-0866

Ride a Mule

The famous Grand Canyon mules are an experience many visitors just cannot miss. You can choose a day trip through the rim forest to The Abyss overlook west of Grand Canyon village. Or, if you want the classic Grand Canyon mule trip, ride the mules down the Bright Angel Trail and spend the night at Phantom Ranch at the bottom of the canyon. Xanterra, a park concessionaire operating by permit from the National Park Service, operates mule trips on Grand Canyon trails.

For further information about mule trips, see Xanterra's website: http://www.grandcanyonlodges.com/things-to-do/mule-trips/.

Running the River

Running the Colorado River through the Grand Canyon is a superb way to explore the canyon's backcountry, and floating the river with modern equipment is safe and easy. There are many excellent day hikes from the river that take you to places that are very difficult to reach from the rims.

Commercial River Trips

You can go on a commercial river trip with a river company operating under permit from the National Park Service. On these trips, professional river guides conduct the river trip, which are a half-day to 18 days in length. Most commercial trips are motorized but some companies offer oar-powered trips. If you have the time, oar-powered trips are the best, because you get to experience both the thrill of the whitewater and the awesome natural quiet of the Grand Canyon on the calm sections of the river between the rapids.

Reservations

To participate in a commercial river trip, make reservations with one of the river companies.

One Day Trips

Half- and full-day river trips start from Lees Ferry at the head of Marble Canyon, and float through lower Glen Canyon, the section of the Colorado River between Glen Canyon Dam and Lees Ferry. While not part of Grand Canyon, Glen Canyon is visually stunning, and there is no white water on this trip. For more information, see Wilderness River Adventure's website: www.riveradventures.com.com, or call 800-992-8022.

Other one day river trips start from Diamond Creek in the western Grand Canyon and end at Grand Canyon West. For information on these whitewater trips, see the Grand Canyon West website: GrandCanyonWest.com, or call 888-868-9378 or 928-769-2636.

Three to 18 Day River Trips

These river trips all launch from Lees Ferry at the head of Marble Canyon. While the oar-powered rafts, motorized rafts, or dories float the entire length of the Grand Canyon to Lake Mead, trip participants can run shorter segments of the Colorado River by hiking the South Kaibab Trail to join or leave a river trip at Phantom Ranch in the eastern canyon.

Another option is to be picked up or dropped off by helicopter at Whitmore Wash in the western canyon. Flights from Whitmore Wash take river runners to Bar Ten Ranch, a private, working cattle ranch, where visitors may stay overnight and then fly out from the ranch airstrip.

Commercial River Companies

For information on river trips starting from Lees Ferry, contact one of the commercial outfitters:

Aramark-Wilderness River Adventures, P.O. Box 717, Page, AZ 86040; 800-992-8022, 928-645-3296, FAX 928-645-6113, www.riveradventures.com

Arizona Raft Adventures, Inc., 4050 E. Huntington Drive, Flagstaff, AZ 86004; 800-786-RAFT, 928-526-8200, FAX 928-526-8246, azraft.com

Arizona River Runners, Inc., P.O. Box 47788, Phoenix, AZ 85068-7788; 800-477-7238, 602-867-4866, FAX 602-867-2174, http://raftarizona.com/

Canyon Explorations and Expeditions, P.O. Box 310, Flagstaff, AZ 86002; 800-654-0723, 928-774-4559, FAX 928-774-4655, www.canyonexplorations.com/

Canyoneers, Inc., P.O. Box 2997, Flagstaff, AZ 86003; 800-525-0924, 928-526-0924, FAX 928-527-9398, www.canyoneers.com/

Colorado River & Trail Expeditions, Inc., P.O. Box 57575, Salt Lake City, UT 84157-0575; 800-253-7328, 801-261-1789, FAX 801-268-1193, www.crateinc.com/

Grand Canyon Expeditions Company, P.O. Box 0, Kanab, UT 84741; 800-544-2691, 435-644-2691,http://www.gcex.com/

Grand Canyon Whitewater, P.O. Box 1300, Page, AZ 86040; 800-343-3121, 928-645-8866, FAX 928-645-9536, www.grandcanyonwhitewater.com/

Hatch River Expeditions, Inc., 5348 E. Burris Ln, Flagstaff, AZ 86004; 800-856-8966, 928-526-4700, FAX: 928-536-4703, http://www.hatchriverexpeditions.com/

O.A.R.S. Grand Canyon, Inc., P.O. Box 67, Angels Camp, CA 95222; 800-346-6277, 209-736-2924, FAX 209-736-2902, www.oars.com

Outdoors Unlimited, 6900 Townsend Winona Road, Flagstaff, AZ 86004; 800-637-7238, FAX 928-526-6185, www.outdoorsunlimited.com

Tour West, Inc., P.O. Box 333, Orem, UT 84059; 800-453-9107, 801-225-0755, FAX 801-225-7979,http://www.twriver.com/

Western River Expeditions, Inc., 7258 Racquet Club Drive, Salt Lake City, UT 84121; 866-904-1160, FAX 801-942-8514, www.westernriver.com

The park maintains a current list of authorized outfitters at www.nps.gov/grca/planyourvisit/river-concessioners.htm

Private River Trips

If you have the experience and the equipment, you can organize a private river trip of 3 to 25 days in length. Private trips are almost always oar-powered. Remember that the Colorado River through Grand Canyon is a technical run with many large, difficult rapids, and that river conditions change radically with water levels.

Permits

Private river trips require a permit which is issued via a lottery system. The lottery is necessary because the demand for permits far exceeds the number of permits available.

Three to Five Day River Trips

The shortest private river trips launch from Diamond Creek, which is located in the western Grand Canyon on the Hualapai Indian Reservation. Permits are required from both the Hualapai Tribe, which owns the access road and put-in, and the National Park Service (the Colorado River is in the national park).

For more information, see the National Park Service Diamond Creek website:
www.nps.gov/grca/planyourvisit/overview-diamond-ck.htm

12 to 25 Day River Trips

These trips all launch from Lees Ferry at the head of Marble Canyon, and end at Diamond Creek in the western Grand Canyon, or at South Cove on Lake Mead below the Grand Canyon.

For more information on private trips starting from Lee's Ferry, see the park website, Private River Trips from Lees Ferry: www.nps.gov/grca/planyourvisit/overview-lees-ferry-diamond-ck.htm

Support Companies for Private River Trips:
www.nps.gov/grca/planyourvisit/river_support.htm

Additional information on both commercial and private river trips can be found on the Park website:
www.nps.gov/grca/planyourvisit/whitewater-rafting.htm

Exploring Further

Some visitors take a short look at the Canyon from a rim viewpoint, and they're done. But others become fascinated by this unique place and want to learn more. Hundreds of books have been written on the Grand Canyon, and many of them are now classics. I'd like to humbly suggest one of my other books as a starting point, *Grand Canyon Guide*. Like this book, *Grand Canyon Guide* is available both in paperback and as a Kindle ebook. Unlike this book, *Grand Canyon Guide* has maps for all the hikes as well as many photos. The paperback has a black and white interior, while the Kindle ebook is in full color. The ebook was designed to be readable on E Ink Kindle book readers, color Fire tablets, and with the free Kindle reading app, on PCs, Macs, iPhones, Android, Blackberry, and Windows Phone devices.

Grand Canyon Guide features a section devoted to further exploration of the Canyon, with more information on the national park and the national monument, as well as the natural history, geology, and human history of the area. There's also an extensive list of books, maps, and videos at the back of the book for those who wish to continue learning about the Grand Canyon.

Also have a look at *Grand Canyon National Park Pocket Guide*. This small FalconGuide is in full color and has unique pop-out maps. It's available as a pocket-size hardback only.

Finally, check out my website, GrandCanyonGuide.net, which was designed to complement my books. The site has up to date news that affects visitors to the Grand Canyon area, as well as general information on the Canyon. There is an extensive list of books, maps, and videos that I recommend under the "Resources" tab.

Before You Go

Please consider leaving a review for this book on Amazon at http://amzn.to/24hobKv. I would greatly appreciate it.

And, if you want to be the first to know about my new books, as well as revisions, consider signing up for my mailing list at eepurl.com/bPW7dD. This list will only be used for that purpose- I will NEVER spam you or share the list with anyone. You can unsubscribe at any time.

About the Author

The author has a serious problem- he doesn't know what he wants to do when he grows up. Meanwhile, he's done such things as wildland fire fighting, running a mountain shop, flying airplanes, shooting photos, and writing books. He's a backcountry skier, climber, figure skater, mountain biker, amateur radio operator, river runner, and sea kayaker- but the thing that really floats his boat is hiking and backpacking. No matter what else he tries, the author always comes back to hiking- especially long, rough, cross-country trips in places like the Grand Canyon. Some people never learn. But what little he has learned, he's willing to share with you- via his books, of course, but also via his websites, blogs, and whatever works

Also by the Author

Books

The Complete 2015 User's Guide to the Amazing Amazon Kindle Fire (with Stephen Windwalker)

The Complete 2015 User's Guide to the Amazing Amazon Kindle - E Ink Edition (with Stephen Windwalker)

Publish! How To Publish Your Book as an E-Book on the Amazon Kindle and in Print with CreateSpace

Grand Canyon Guide: Your Complete Guide to the Grand Canyon Region

Exploring With GPS: A Practical Field Guide for Satellite Navigation

Exploring Great Basin National Park: Including Mount Moriah Wilderness

Google Nexus 2013: Making Your Android Tablet Work for You

Running Android: Using Your Phone and Tablet for Work and Play

Websites

BruceGrubbs.com

BrightAngelPress.com

ExploringGreatBasin.net

ExploringGrandCanyon.info

ExploringGps.com

FlagstaffFigureSkatingClub.com

Blogs

Get Out and Stay Out: bruce-grubbs.blogspot.com

Travels With Kindle: http://travelswithkindle.blogspot.com

Social

linkedin.com/in/brucegrubbs

facebook.com/bruce.grubbs.outdoor.author

twitter.com/grandcynwriter

Index

Made in the USA
San Bernardino, CA
21 February 2020

64791416R00073